MEDITAT
WORKBC

MEDITATION WORKBOOK

A Practical Guide to Doing It *Your* Way

GREER ALLICA

BURNS & OATES

Published in Great Britain in 1991 by
Burns & Oates Limited,
Wellwood, North Farm Road,
Tunbridge Wells, Kent TN2 3DR.

Originally published in Australia by
David Lovell Publishing
Brunswick, Victoria 3056

Cover design by Peter Shaw
Illustrations throughout by Melva Fitzallen
Designed by Peter Shaw
Photographs on front and back covers by Bill Thomas
Typeset by Peritech Pty. Ltd., Blackburn Victoria
Printed in Australia by Globe Press, Brunswick Victoria

The lines on page v are from Four Quartets
by T.S. Eliot, reprinted by permission
of Faber and Faber Ltd. London

ISBN: 0 86012 193 3

Cover illustration: embroidered mandala by
Catherine Blackman
'The mandala is a magical circle—a symbolic
representation of mental and spiritual renewal. The
pure white centre is the energy source—focus of
highest conscious awareness. The butterfly,
representing transformation, comes to the flower,
symbol of the self in psychological wholeness. Purple
—a meditative healing colour—and yellow—representing
wisdom and creative thought—are opposites in the
spectrum. Two opposites make a whole, indicating
transformation, wholeness, awareness and growth.
Radiating energy flows from the centre to the outer,
and back to the innermost central point.'

In order to arrive at what you do not know
You must go by a way which is the way of ignorance.
In order to possess what you do not possess
You must go by the way of dispossession.
In order to arrive at what you are not
You must go through the way in which you are not.
And what you do not know is the only thing you know
And what you own is what you do not own
And where you are is where you are not.

T. S. Eliot

Integration means the creation of an inner unity, a centre of strength and freedom, so that the being ceases to be a mere object, acted upon by outside forces, and becomes a subject, acting from its own 'inner space' into the space outside itself.

E. F. Schumacher

With gratitude and appreciation for all my mentors and supporters, I share this knowledge that has changed my life, in the hope that it will be a source of inspiration for others.

I dedicate this book to all seekers. May they find and manifest the beauty within themselves.

And to my children — Bronwyn, Robert and Mirren — I dedicate this book as a token of my faith in their future and in a future peace.

Contents

AUTHOR'S NOTE

The art of meditation is the act of letting go—letting go of the limitations of the body, of the mind, and of the emotions.

To do this one must, paradoxically, learn to *control* these elements so that the meditative state can be brought on at will when it is most needed. This is where you might begin.

The ideal, of course, is to live meditation so that every moment is one of peace, balance and harmony — even in the midst of their opposites.

For myself, meditation has been a way of discovering and coming to terms with who I am. I began it in response to a need: to cope with stress and trauma in my life. The rewards of meditation have been enormous — it has been a beautiful and fulfilling experience and has made my life easier, less complicated, so much more enjoyable and, most of all, more *fun*.

I once wrote a poem that expresses the art of being, which is what meditation is, in essence — the link between the seen and the unseen, effort and non-effort, holding on and letting go . . . getting in touch with the flow of life, and going with it.

LIGHT

Light-travels
of water
across shadow islands,
blushing reeds
stroking, the wavering roots
unravel down
and part of you is found.
Light races
to the hard, clay crusts of land
in the dense olive bushes
under the grey gums;
look at the solid banks —
where did it begin?
where did it end?
what can I grasp?
Suddenly
gold pussy-willow leaves
float down, laughing
with the water move away;
and part of you is found.

Introduction

Meditation Workbook is an attempt to de-mystify meditation, to make it accessible to everyone for, despite what you might have heard, *meditation is not difficult.*

Approach this book with a sense of anticipation, discovery, excitement. I expect you will read it many times; that there will be parts of it that you refer to again and again; and that ultimately it will be a stepping stone from which you move to a greater personal integration.

This book will undoubtedly be one among many that you will read about meditation and related areas. The deeper you move into the subject area the wider and more all-encompassing you will find that it becomes.

But meditation is, above all, *practical* — it must be practised to be mastered. No matter how extensive your reading, it will never supplant the energy and commitment you must put into actually doing it. *Meditation Workbook* is your companion to doing it!

Each chapter can be read on its own and does not depend on the other chapters for your comprehension. At the same time the effect of the whole book is cumulative. As you read more of it the parts will come together to make greater sense. By the end of the book you will have a more complete understanding of the complexities of meditation than you did at the beginning.

I suggest that the best way to read this book is to read the whole book one or more times, then return to the area on which you wish to concentrate. For example, you might return to the chapter on breath, re-read it and work with it on a practical level for several months. The exercises are meant to be done not just once, but again and again. Awareness is not achieved instantly but is a gradual process. Explore the breath thoroughly by giving yourself time. Don't limit yourself only to this book, or to books in general as the sole medium of learning. For instance you will learn a lot about breathing and the body by taking classes in Yoga, Tai-Chi or the Feldenkrais Method.

If it is difficult to find the time for this practical exploration, if you don't feel disciplined enough to begin, if it all seems like hard work — then make it fun as I did by joining with a few similarly interested friends to form a meditation group. It is not necessary to have an inspired leader or guru. Meet and meditate regularly, perhaps once a week, working through the exercises in the book. After your regular meditation together you can enjoy supper and discussion. At other times you will be able to go to workshops and lectures together.

The bonding that you form with a group such as this is both stimulating and supportive, and the energy of a group meditating is so much stronger than that of a lone meditator. Meditation within the group will also motivate you to do it on your own, because you will have found that you actually enjoy doing it, that you *want* to do it.

Don't expect to move into deep meditation overnight. Be patient with yourself. As you continue with the process the rewards will become obvious and you will want to pursue meditation for its own sake. But until you get to the point where meditation creates its own momentum, you must persist. Be reassured that even experienced meditators sometimes have unsuccessful meditations.

Learning to meditate is rather like learning any other skill. For example, when you learn to drive a car, you are at first very much aware of all the things you have to work in order to operate it — gears, pedals, steering wheel, indicators, lights. There is also the external environment: other cars, road conditions, street signs, pedestrians, traffic lights. You are aware of all these things separately. It seems at first an impossible task to assimilate and co-ordinate them all. But after persistent practice you become an accomplished driver. All those separate elements which were once so prominent and confusing now blend into one integral activity — and driving becomes automatic.

So it is with meditation.

ONE

Transforming the senses

The simplest way to begin is with your body — simply because you are always with it. To be in tune with your body you must first understand the relationship between the physical body, breathing, emotions and your mental state. None of these acts independently; the breath affects the blood circulation and consequently the amount of oxygen going to all organs of the body. If your body is not working effectively it influences your mood and your thoughts. If you are thinking negative thoughts, then you are also feeling them, and the rate of breathing alters accordingly.

To know this connection on a mental level is one thing but to understand it thoroughly on a deeper level is another. Let's suppose you are angry. In the course of experiencing this emotion you may have a fleeting image of yourself in this state; you may perhaps notice that you are out of breath, that your chest feels tight or that you have a pain in the stomach. You might only be in touch with those rationalizing thoughts that justify your anger to yourself.

To be familiar with any one of the above factors is an indication of awareness, but on its own each tells you very little. Knowing of the relationship between all of these, seeing the whole, requires you to be very much in touch with yourself. The process of learning about yourself, listening to yourself, requires time and persistence, and a willingness to turn off outside stimuli. This last is the most difficult and elusive task and is the reason why people turn to learning meditation.

How, initially, do you make contact with these outside stimuli? It is through the five senses of smell, touch, taste, seeing and hearing. The senses act rather like transducers in first receiving a sensation, then setting up a reaction which affects particular parts of the body and then spreads. And of course the mind, the emotions, the breath, are involved in the whole assimilation process. The transforming effect can be magnified by working from the outer sense to the inner sense. For example, I use my physical sense of smell to let my mind 'imagine' the sense of smell, so that it becomes as real in my imagination. This does not mean a suspension of reality - more a heightening of my own awareness.

Though in practice all five senses rely on and work with each other, it is helpful to examine each sense on its own for the purpose of self exploration.

SMELL

Outer

I can smell external things in the world like roses, lemons, coffee or spices. I think I *know* how they smell, because I have smelt them before and because I can compare them with other like or unlike smells. Some smells are easily categorized as either pleasant (eg roses) or unpleasant (eg garbage) but others (say, mushrooms) are more dependent on individual associations and preferences.

Inner

Can I now take this sense and use it to help me imagine a rose, or a lemon? By using my memory, can I capture the *essence* of the smell of each, and hold it in my mind? This requires focusing and concentration.

We talk about a dog being able to 'smell' fear in a human; its sense of smell is indeed acute. The fear it homes in on is the result of particular changes in the person's body, the emotions and the mind — the body perhaps sweats and tenses; the breathing becomes quicker as fear is felt; and thoughts, often conflicting, run through the mind. "I remember that my mother was bitten by a dog when I was a little girl"; "I must pretend I am not scared"; "He looks very fierce . . . maybe I should throw something at him".

Sensing intangibles like fear involves a combination of all senses, of which the sense of smell is one. This sense, though underdeveloped in civilised humans, can be expanded by working on the *inner* sense.

TOUCH

Outer

I can touch something prickly—perhaps a prickly plant — and something smooth—like a baby's skin — and feel the difference. I can feel textures:

moistness or dryness, heat or cold, thickness or thinness. I touch with different emotions, perhaps love, or hatred.

As I become more familiar with the variety of sensations and the differences between them I am more able to reach the inner sense.

Inner

I translate the outer awareness of touch to an inner awareness by bringing back its *memory*. By using the memory of what it is to touch a particular thing, I make it more accessible and more real in my mind. I explore every aspect of what I remember.

Intangibles? We talk about 'touching someone's heart' or 'soul' which means that we have had sufficient empathy to *reach through* to that person's very depths. This surely is an example of using the inner sense of touch which, in turn, will make our outer lives more real.

And fear? If we are afraid, and don't recognize or admit our fear, we tend to shrink from another's touch; we protect ourselves by stiffening the body, like an armour.

TASTE

Outer

Taste and smell are inextricably linked, one sense influencing the other. I can taste whether coffee is strong or weak; that is, the *density* of its taste. I can taste dryness or sweetness, bitterness or saltiness, spiciness.

Inner

If I can recall the taste of coffee and concentrate on experiencing the memory of its taste, then it can be as real to me as if I were actually drinking it.

Fear. Can you taste fear? Think back to a time when you were afraid. Try to recapture that moment and be aware of what was happening inside you. What happened to your saliva—was there more or less of it? Were your lips dry or moist? Of course your senses were working together.

SEEING

Outer

I can see different colours, the difference between blue sky and brown/green trees; the varying tones of green within the trees. I can see shapes and movement, and the way colours change and blur as objects move.

The colours that we see are only a small part of the electromagnetic spectrum and are made up of vibrations which vary in wavelength according to the particular colour.

Inner

'A black mood'—you must know the expression. Some people who have already developed their sense of sight may indeed be aware of changing colours around a person, as her mood changes. This is a special gift and is a development of this particular sense.

To shut your eyes and visualize the exact colours of the trees and of the sky around you is a good exercise to develop this inner sense. Every time you lose the mind picture open your eyes again till you think you have memorized it.

Fear? It is not difficult to see fear in another person's face when they are afraid—the pupils of the eyes dilate and the facial muscles tighten.

HEARING

Outer

I can hear the sounds of bird calls, the sound of another's voice, the noise of a jet, the soft sounds of wind whispering among trees, the ripple of water over stones.

Although in this age we are assaulted by sound from all directions we have developed the capacity to choose what we want to hear and 'tune out' on the rest.

Inner

The inner sense of hearing involves not only a recall of familiar sounds, but an opening or freeing of ourselves that we might hear 'the sounds that are not sounds'. We need to be both receptive and perceptive, to be combining all our senses, to hear the words behind words.

For example, if a person says 'I love you' but their body is tight and their arms stiff, then what we actually hear differs from what we 'hear' on the inside.

To increase our perception in this way, it is good to begin first with the sounds we know, to recreate them in our minds—their pitch, tone and intensity—till they are as real as the outer sound.

Fear? Fear translates into the voice: the fever-pitch shriek and quickened, frantic breathing can both be heard. Can you also hear the changed beat of your heart when you have been frightened by something?

SELF SPACE

Here now is the space you create for yourself in this book, and in your daily life. Repeat to yourself as often as you can, one or some of the following affirmations:

'Every day I make a space for myself.'

'I now give myself permission to create space in my day, for me.'

'As I care, so I share, time with myself each day.'

'Because I matter, I give myself time and attention each day.'

'I am in touch with all my senses — both outer and inner.'

Write the affirmations again and again on a piece of paper that you can pin up somewhere prominent.

Transforming the senses

Take as long as you feel you need to work on transforming your senses, from a limited consciousness to an expanded awareness.

This is your aim to make a bridge with your mind from the outer, to the inner, or higher consciousness.

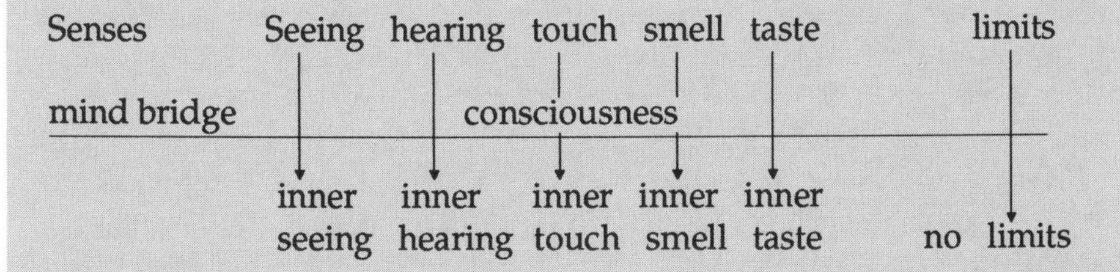

Your methods are described below.

Mirror of nature

Find a quiet and beautiful place in nature. Sit down and close your eyes for a minute; as you take a long breath *out*, feel as if you are totally emptying yourself. Imagine that you are a deep reflective mirror. Now open your eyes, and as you breath *in*, absorb all the sensual impressions around you. When you are confident that your mirror holds the picture exactly as you see it, shut your eyes and explore the scene, going through each sense, in your mind. If you want to reinforce any details, open your eyes for a time before returning once again to your mirror.

Try doing this exercise initially for about five minutes, increasing the time as you improve your concentration and visualization.

Fruit exploration

Sit somewhere inside where there are few external distractions.

Take a piece of fruit and hold it in your hands. Concentrate entirely on this fruit, exploring first what you see, feel, touch and smell, even taste. Now close your eyes, take a deep breath and using the same senses try to go with your mind, inside the fruit. Use your imagination to capture totally the essence of the fruit, to come to 'know' it more fully. This is not a case of swapping identities and trying to become the fruit; more a breaking down of the barriers that prevent you from understanding the identity of something else. As the focus is shifted from self to fruit, self, though never lost, becomes a background feature and your awareness expands leading to an *opening* of self.

Sound synthesis

Go somewhere where you know there will be sound—this could be traffic, music, bird or animal calls. Sit comfortably with your eyes shut and listen intently to the sounds; so intently that after a while this is the only thing occupying your mind. Explore every aspect of the sound, feel it reverberate inside you. After a while you will notice a change. The sound will no longer be an intrusion on your consciousness; you will no longer even be aware of hearing it, even though you know it is there. Your heartbeat will have slowed down, your breathing will be both lighter and slower, and a sense of calm and peace will fill you.

Taste sensations

First put some lemon juice, then salt, then honey on your tongue and notice the differences between them. Now, taking it more slowly, taste each again, more deliberately. Take note of the smell, appearance, texture, taste; first on the tip of the tongue, then further back on the palate. See how far you can be aware of the taste sensation as it passes down the gullet and into the stomach.

After completing all three, try now to recreate (by remembering) all three, one after the other, using only your mind.

Flower power
Prepare a vase of beautiful, perfumed flowers. Sit in front of it, preferably on a straight-backed chair with your spine erect, your head slightly bent and your feet flat on the floor, legs apart. Now, breathing in deeply, focus intently on the flowers; notice the different colours, shapes and textures, the number and placement of petals and stamens. Notice the difference between petal and stem. Absorb the perfume.

Now shut your eyes and, as you breathe in, recall every sensual detail. When you lose the flowers in your head, open your eyes and memorize them once more.

As you become more expert with this exercise you will find that you are using your five senses simultaneously. You will also learn to coordinate the breath with the senses so that you have the sensation of 'breathing in' the flowers. 'Flower Power' can also be done with a single flower stem.

MEDITATION DIARY

Keep a meditation diary in which you record your perceptions and feelings.

Note any changes that occur. For example:

Fruit Exploration . . .

8/6 trying this for the first time I used an apple. Pleased that I could hold the red colour when I shut my eyes. . .the colour stayed in my mind longer than the shape. Couldn't really go INSIDE the apple though — too difficult.

15/7 Have been trying this apple thing for a while now and always seem to get stuck when I try to go inside the fruit. So thought I'd try an orange today. Success! I could really feel it — the moistness, the tiny hair-like fibres. Perhaps I'll go swimming in it next time! For a moment I really forgot myself.

Make a note too of the things you have found most difficult, after doing the various exercises. Try to define the areas of difficulty. Perhaps you have found that one of your senses is not nearly as sharply tuned as the others. Look at this and relate it to your life. For example, if it is hearing, ask yourself, 'Do I really listen to people properly?' 'Is there something about myself which I'm refusing to hear (to know and understand)?'

This is the sort of sensitivity which will emerge after practice of the exercises. 'My outer senses lead me to my inner senses; my inner senses lead me to a greater understanding and awareness of all things.'

TWO

Body Blocks

You have now used your five senses to explore your body and to move beyond it to the inner senses. By doing so, you will have become more familiar with and more sensitive to your own body and its capacities.

As you did some of the exercises in chapter one, you may have noticed certain difficulties in both perception and concentration which relate both to the body and to the mind. Chapter four deals with the mind; here we will discuss body blocks.

It is ironic that just at the very moment we decide to become quiet within, our body lets us know that it is there. This is where the problems arise, for in order to meditate we must move *beyond* our awareness of the body. Described below are some of the body blocks you may experience, together with some suggested ways to release them, so that you can begin your meditation in a state of relaxation.

BODY SENSATIONS

Just as a naughty child will persist in bad behaviour until we give him our full attention, so does the body persist in telling us by a pain, a muscle twitch, a stomach rumble, a tickling sensation, a sneeze, a cramp, that it wants our full and undivided attention.

The way to 'lose' your body is to fill your mind exclusively with an awareness of it. If it is a tickle in the left thigh that is worrying you, don't try to ignore or repress it. That is the worst thing you can do; by bringing it into the full focus of your mind and concentrating on this alone, you gradually train your mind to gain control. After a while the tickle will subside and cease to exist.

Don't let the mind wander

It is tempting to let the mind stray away from the particular body sensation which you are experiencing. As you feel the tickle in your left thigh, thoughts begin to flood your mind. You remember the last time you felt ticklish and that some people say that it's a form of self protection; you wonder when the rest of your body will start to itch, then suddenly feel that you will have to open your eyes, sit up and scratch yourself; you wonder how to control this impulse; you think people might be noticing that you are twitching; you start wondering about people in general; how you always think that others are noticing or are more interested in you than they really are — and there it is! You're off on an undisciplined ramble that has nothing to do with making you feel more peaceful, relaxed and centred.

When this happens don't chastise yourself (guilt doesn't help the relaxation process) but bring your mind gently back — in this case, to the sensation of the tickle.

External irritations

There are some external irritations which seem to force the body to take note, and so detract from any attempts to relax. Maybe it is a fly buzzing round the room or alighting on your nose; the play of light and shadow across your closed eyes; a fire engine, or a thunderstorm outside; the hardness of the floor on which you are lying; or maybe a door creaking.

If you continue to be bothered by any of these things or another similar irritation, focus on it until it begins to fade into the background. After teaching yourself to do this, you will eventually find it easier simply to shift your focus while still being aware of the distraction, but placing it in the background. There will then be no need to put your energies into concentrating on what bothers you.

Another method of dealing with external irritations is to create a protective barrier around yourself. Visualize a layer of light around your body and, on the outside of this, an impenetrable gold barrier. While you remain aware of the particular distraction, you don't allow it to penetrate your personal space. This can be most effective but a lot depends on the strength of your powers of visualization.

You might wonder how you can be aware of distractions and still meditate. It is not true to say (as so many think) that a meditator is in a world of her own, completely oblivious to everything else. Meditation is more an absolute *super awareness*, where the mind becomes so powerful that its particular focus can be shifted at will or where, alternatively, the mind can bring numerous separate elements into focus and synthesize them. In either case the net result is a conception of oneness and wholeness.

RELAXING THE BODY

Before any meditation it is important to go through a series of steps to relax the body. Ideally, lie down on your back with your legs slightly apart, arms not touching the body, and palms upwards. If this is not comfortable, sit in a straight-backed chair with feet apart and flat on the floor, hands on knees either with palms downward or open, with thumb and forefinger lightly touching. The aim is to be neither too comfortable nor too uncomfortable.

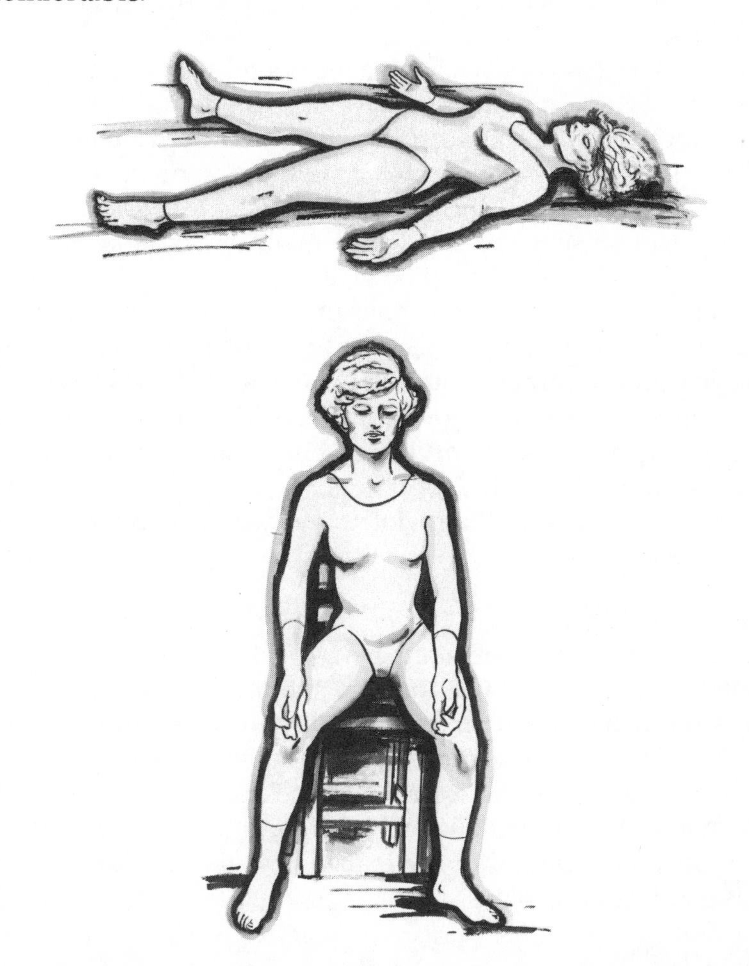

Now take your mind right through your body, noting the areas where you feel most tension. Then follow the sequence outlined below:

1. Concentrate and feel the tension
2. Exaggerate the tension
3. Release the tension
4. Note the difference

Concentrate and feel the tension

You can begin at any area — perhaps the one of which you are most aware — and go from there to cover the entire body, breaking it down to small areas on which the mind can focus. Allow the mind to flow on from one part of the body to another so that the concentration is not broken. For example, if you begin at the stomach, move out from there to hips and buttocks, or chest. Alternatively, you can begin at the top of the head, or the tip of the toes.

As you feel the tension in each area, go progressively through the four steps, before moving on to the next area of tension. Use the five senses to help you experience the state of your body, and to evaluate muscle tension. You will probably notice after repeating the process several times, that one particular part of the body is consistently tense. This then is where you *store* tension (perhaps over many years) and is the area to which particular attention should be given. At this stage concentrate only on the physical. As you become more practised, you will probably want to go further in exploring the storage areas of tension and their emotional/psychological components, which will be discussed later.

As your mind passes through your body you might see different colours which give an indication of the level of tension in that area. Red, orange, brown, and black all reflect high tension levels, either physical and/or emotional. Green, blue, violet, and white reflect a more relaxed and peaceful state.

Exaggerate the tension

From the present level of tension that you feel in each part of your body, next progressively tighten and increase the level as far as you can. By doing this you will come to understand the nature of tension in each area, and to realize just how close you have been to its threshhold. It is important to do this as an exercise because in the normal course of events we don't monitor the tension in our body; we learn to live with it till it begins to feel 'normal' and we no longer realize how tense we are nor how relaxed it is possible to become.

Release the tension

Having now tensed each muscle in your body to its maximum capacity, slowly release the tension. Don't try to release tension from the whole body all in one go but, as you did before, use your mind to pass through each part of the body, letting go. If you try to think 'I *must* release, I *must* relax', it will be more difficult. Imagine instead the tension just flowing out, or lifting off, with each part of your body becoming lighter and lighter. If you can also visualize the colour (red?) and shape (sparks?) of this nervous energy, then releasing it may be easier.

Note the difference
You have experienced a state of extreme tension and also a state of complete absence of tension. Rather than being a progression, the steps towards relaxation must now be brought together so that while you are in a state of relaxation, you can still recall the *memory* of tension in every bone, organ and muscle of your body. In this way a comparison can be made. As you then come to understand fully the difference between the two states, each future relaxation will be easier and will become a triggered response. The memory of sliding from tension, to release to relaxation, will bring about an instant change in the body.

When you have completed the four steps throughout the different parts of the body, make a mental sweep over the whole body once more, checking that no area has tightened up again.

From this state of relaxation you can now feel yourself becoming lighter and lighter and drifting higher and further away from the body. In order to imagine that feeling of lightness you may need to feel a corresponding heaviness of the physical body. The body is released and you begin to meditate either by remaining in this floating mind*less* state, or by using your mind further to visualize *(see chapter five).*

EMOTIONS

You may notice as you go through the relaxation steps that one particular area holds more tension than others. This is also the area where you are holding an emotion or emotions. We call it a 'locked-in emotion', because it has been stored there for some period of time, and because ordinary methods of release (e.g. exercise) have not been sufficient to release it.

While you are in a relaxed state, think about this area of your body and the reasons why you might have chosen this site to store your tension. Of course your conscious mind sees no reason at all for holding tension, but the subconscious mind is aware and this is the depth to which you must reach.

Me and my stomach

Let us take an example. I have found that my stomach is my tension area and is always the first area to respond in any difficult situation. I begin to think about all my associations with stomach — 'food, fat, full up', 'fat Aunt Edith', 'indulgence, repulsive', 'I can't stomach it'. It is likely that this sort of free association will lead you on from one thought to another until one word acts as a trigger for the deeper realisation — 'I can't stomach it'. What can't I stomach? I remember how I'm always conscious that this part of my body might be sticking out and is unattractive. I try to isolate the emotion connected with all these thoughts. Is it anger? Why am I angry? What am I angry about? Is it fear? What am I frightened of?

Now that I have *begun* to understand my tension area, I try asking myself the same questions when I am *in the middle of exaggerating the tension* in my stomach. This time I might be acutely aware of a rush of emotions; perhaps a scene will come into my mind that causes me to relive anger, or fear. I have the opportunity now to look at other people, other perspectives connected with this scene, and to come to new understandings.

It may take several sessions to work through an emotional block. It may require using other methods of release such as hitting into a pillow or screaming the anger into words (obviously in a place and time where you have privacy and know you will not be interrupted). Then after such negative emotions have been expressed there is the process of forgiveness of yourself and of others.

You will know that you have released your emotional block when tension no longer collects in that same area.

The example given above is necessarily a simplified example of the whole process; your emotional reactions, your blocking mechanisms are more complex but this is the method by which you can come to some understanding, and relaxation of the body should then be easier.

Self-discovery is usually gradual; as more hidden parts of yourself begin to surface you will realize the big part that the mind plays in creating emotional blocks. Thoughts and emotions about a particular experience which repeats itself in our lives, are based on belief systems which we've formed in our minds from a very early age.

So, a body block must be approached from all angles, if it is to be dissolved.

SELF SPACE

Create some space for yourself in the day, to try these relaxation techniques and to explore your own body blocks. First, some affirmations:

'I now give myself permission to spend time on myself'

'I allow myself to relax; I am willing to release.'

Progressive body relaxation

There are many tapes available now which work on progressively relaxing the body through tensing and then releasing the tension. Sometimes while you are a beginner it is *easier* to have something external, but it is certainly not necessary. Some people like to put their own voice on tape; others may find that a soothing piece of music in the background is an aid to relaxation. See page 22 for a list of suitable tapes.

Relaxation technique
Find a comfortable place in which to lie on your back (a carpeted floor is a good place; no pillows if possible) or sit in a straight-backed chair. Make sure that the room is warm or cover yourself with a blanket, since the body temperature drops appreciably when you are in a state of deep relaxation.

Now, breathing into each part of the body on which you are focusing, begin with the head. The breathing helps you with the first step in your relaxation sequence: concentrate and feel the tension. Follow with exaggerating the tension, releasing the tension and noting the difference — repeating this process.

Your mind passes through the hair, over the surface of the skull, across the forehead and the eyebrows, behind the eyes, the cheeks, the temples, the jawbone, the ears. Travel in and around and through. Then down the throat, the back of the neck, and across to the shoulders. Feel the tension, exaggerate, release, and note the difference. Now down one arm and then the other, dividing the arm into upper and lower; then into the hands and the fingers.

Going back up the arm, to the neck, pass down the spine through the vertebrae, and back up again. Move into the heart, the ribs and the lungs behind; down to the stomach, intestines, and then from the hipbone travelling down one leg and then the other, through thigh, calf and shin to the feet and finally the toes.

Concentration is easier if the progression is smooth, flowing from one part and connecting to the next, rather than jumping from head to toes, or arms to stomach. Imagine that you are drawing a continuous line with one starting point and one end. This would be the progression.

Head
throat
shoulders
arms
hands
spine
heart
ribs

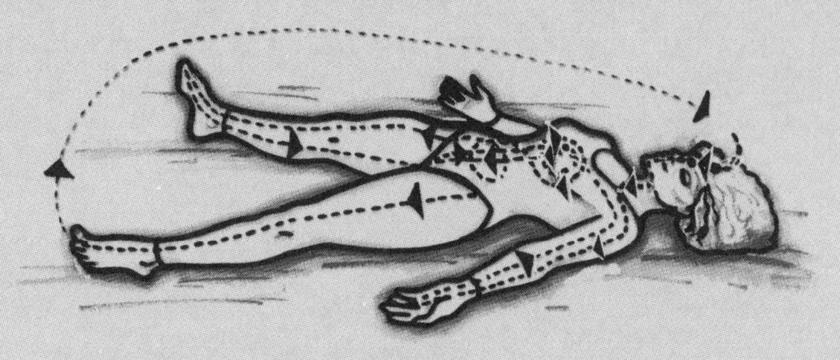

lungs
stomach
intestines
hips
legs
feet
toes

The heavy body technique

Because the body has a density and a mass, tension can be released simply by feeling into the heaviness of each part of the body, and allowing it to become even heavier, to a point where it seems to drop away, and you are left correspondingly lighter. From this state of lightness, you can then drift into meditation.

This technique is best done lying flat on the floor as previously described. Prepare yourself first by vigourous stretching and yawning. Then use the following script:

I surrender myself. (*slight pause*)

My right arm is heavy . . . my right hand is heavy . . . my right arm and hand are heavy . . . my right arm and hand are sinking into the ground. (*Pause*)

My left arm is heavy . . . my left hand is heavy . . . my left arm and hand are heavy . . . my left arm and hand are sinking into the ground. (*Pause*)

I surrender myself. (*slight pause*)

My right leg is heavy . . . my right foot is heavy . . . my right leg and foot are heavy . . . my right leg and foot are sinking into the ground. (*pause*)

My left leg is heavy . . . my left foot is heavy . . . my left leg and foot are heavy . . . my left leg and foot are sinking into the ground. (*pause*)

I surrender myself. (*slight pause*)

My arms are heavy . . . my legs are heavy . . . my arms and legs are heavy . . . my arms and legs are sinking into the ground. (*pause*)

I surrender myself. (*slight pause*)

My head is heavy . . . my eyes are sinking into their sockets . . . my tongue and jaw are heavy . . . my whole head is heavy . . . my whole head is sinking into the ground. (*pause*)

I surrender myself. (*slight pause*)

My neck is heavy . . . my shoulders are heavy . . . my neck and shoulders are heavy . . . my neck and shoulders are sinking into the ground. (*pause*)

I surrender myself. (*slight pause*)

My chest is heavy . . . my stomach is heavy . . . my chest and stomach are heavy . . . my chest and stomach are sinking into the ground. (*pause*)

I surrender myself. (*slight pause*)

My back is heavy . . . my whole back is heavy . . . my whole back is sinking into the ground. (*pause*)

I surrender myself. (*slight pause*)

My body is heavy (*pause*)

My body is heavy . . . my body is sinking into the ground (*pause*)

I surrender myself. (*slight pause*) My body is heavy.

As you feel the body dropping away begin to feel light hovering just above the body, then collecting in a bubble over the stomach, and slowly lifting, up and up.

(Based on a more detailed exercise described by Dr Bruno Hans Geba in *Breathe Away Your Tension,* Wildwood House, London, 1974.)

Emotional release

Lie down in a comfortable place and, after going through the body relaxation, place your hands on the stomach area around the navel. You are in contact now with the liver, the spleen, the pancreas, the adrenal glands, all areas that can store negative emotions.

Using the mind and the breath, draw in light from the crown of the head right down to the stomach area. Keep breathing connectedly without any pause between the 'in' and 'out' breath and continue to allow light to pour into the stomach. Be an intent observer; don't let the mind wander.

You may be aware of particular emotions suddenly welling up; as this happens, release them with each 'out' breath. It is important not to identify with the emotion, but rather to allow it to surface and to let go. It may help, as you are breathing out and releasing to repeat to yourself a connected releasing statement such as, 'I release this fear and let it go' or, 'I no longer need this anger — I feel it dissolve through the pores of my skin as I breathe out and let go.'

As you cleanse yourself of these negative emotions visualize the colour orange,the colour of release,and then again fill the stomach area with beautiful golden light, healing and renewing your whole being. Feel a state of peace and calm and repeat internally, 'I am at peace'.

Forgiveness

Invariably a release of negative emotions is coupled with a need to forgive, both yourself and others.

Continue with one hand still on the stomach area and the other hand on the soul centre, just above the heart, in the centre of the body.

Breathing 'light' into this soul centre, visualize the person you are forgiving enveloped in a bubble of light and, connected by a cord to yourself, another bubble of light.

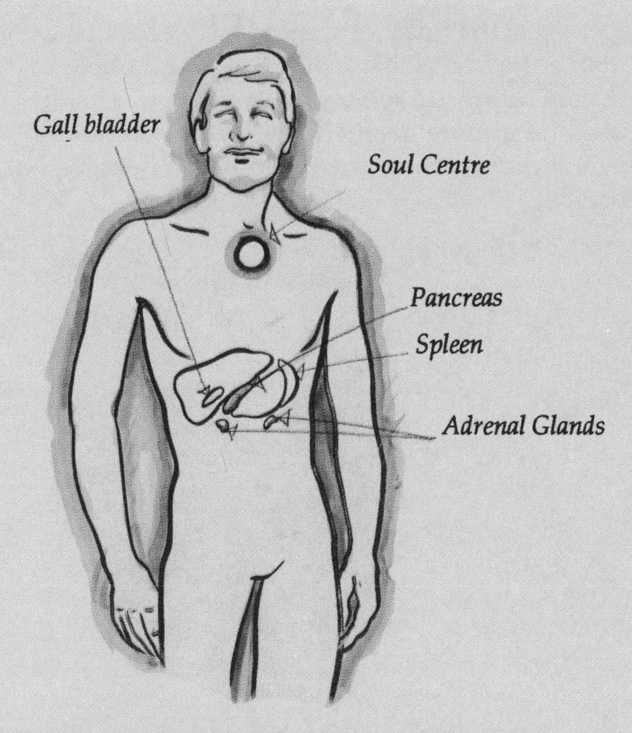

Forgiveness and emotional release centres

As you see the cord break, and the bubbles of light float their separate ways, repeat to yourself: 'I forgive you, (*other person's name*) and release you to your highest good.' Then correspondingly, 'You forgive me, (*your name*) and release me to my highest good.' 'All is well between us and the Universe now.' This is an affirmation which I have found especially useful for forgiveness and release. It is a variation of one used by Catherine Ponder, author of *The Healing Secret of the Ages*. (*See Further Reading*)

It is quite possible that you may also have to forgive your own judgement of yourself, in which case you would add, 'I forgive you (*your own name*) and release you to your highest good' — this, after acknowledging and coming to terms with your own guilt which, quite possibly, was the original motivation for your self-judgement. (*See chapter four*)

MUSIC FOR RELAXATION

While there are many types of 'relaxing' music, for the purposes of a deeper relaxation or meditation, music that is atonal is preferable. Otherwise the rhythmic patterns or the familiarity of the tunes can be distracting. Here are some suggested titles:

Robert Bearns and Ron Dexter *Golden Voyage* (4 vols)
Jon Bernoff and Marcus Allen *Breathe*
Paul Fitzgerald and Mark Flanagan *Quiet Water*
Med Goodall *Emergence*
Steve Halpern *Dawn, Eastern Peace, Spectrum Suite* and others.
Alan Hinde *The Twilight of Dreams*
Paul Horn *In India, The Great Pyramids*
Karma *Ionospheres*
Kitaro *Silk Road, Oasis*
Nicholas Land *Night Echoes*
Patrick O'Hearn *Ancient Dreams*
John Richardson *Cirrus, The Calling*
Mike Rowland *Solace*
Clifford White *Ascension*
Arden Wilken *Inner Focus, Music for Healing, Inner Harmony*

This is not an exhaustive list by any means but merely offers some suggestions.

THREE

The power of the breath

A REVOLUTION IN BREATH

So far, we have discussed briefly the use of breath in relaxing the body and in releasing emotional blocks.

The importance of breathing for both relaxation and meditation, cannot be overemphasized for it is impossible to do either to any effect if the breathing has not been mastered. Indeed, one must almost go through a 'revolution in breath' to reach an understanding of its absolute centrality to meditation.

We all come into life breathing; it is a natural process, and therefore we take it for granted. The disadvantage of this is that we become careless with it, assuming that because it is something that goes on automatically, we don't have any control over it.

It is only when something goes wrong — perhaps with the lungs, or the heart; or asthma conditions — that we begin to take notice of the breathing process, and realize that we *can* control our breathing. It is not necessary to be sick, however, to become aware of the breath; awareness and a change in the way we breathe will bring about health and vitality and become an ongoing preventative measure.

FOCUS ON THE BREATH

Focus on your breathing for a time — listen to it, your pulse and your heartbeat; feel the cool air coming in through the nostrils, and passing out, slightly warmer. See how far you can follow the breath with your mind, imagining it as a silken thread, wafting through the body, and then out again.

Imagine the breath entering every cell in your body, filling it with oxygen and with life-force, surging through the blood and purifying it, making every organ function well and with ease. See the breath as a shaft of light, bringing with it positive, energizing qualities.

As your vision becomes richer and fuller, and both mind and breath work together, so the breathing becomes more effective, more powerful. Try, too, to really feel what is happening — like an inner listening — so that your thoughts are given substance and depth.

The above are all general directions to help you to focus on and familiarize yourself with your breathing. You should be able to find out just where you are up to!

Now, we elaborate on the various ways in which you can utilize the breath — attempting to isolate the steps in the process, a process so tantalizingly simple yet, paradoxically, both complex and esoteric to most people.

Breathing as a preparation for relaxation

Sometimes you may find that you are so wound up, so tense, that it is impossible to settle yourself and proceed to the 'progressive body relaxation'. The body, being so full of tension, refuses to co-operate. In this case, it is a good idea to begin with movement and co-ordinated deep breathing.

Most people use only part of their lungs, usually the middle part, and never fully breathe out. They may also breathe irregularly, holding the breath at times. The body, consequently, ends up not receiving the amounts of fresh oxygen and energy that it could.

The Abdominal Breath

To breathe a really deep breath, we have to reverse the process that most of us have become used to — that is: breathing in, lifting the chest, and caving in the stomach. What we need to do is, breathe in pushing down the diaphragm, so filling the lower part of the lungs, and making the stomach balloon out. As the breath is expelled, the stomach sinks in again and the diaphragm moves up to its original position.

This is the breath used in Yoga, and by athletes, for greater energy and more centredness.

After you have practised this breath and become comfortable with it, you will then be able to combine it with exercise, breathing in with all the expanded (opening out, or stretching) movements, and breathing out with all contracted (closing in, or coming together) movements.

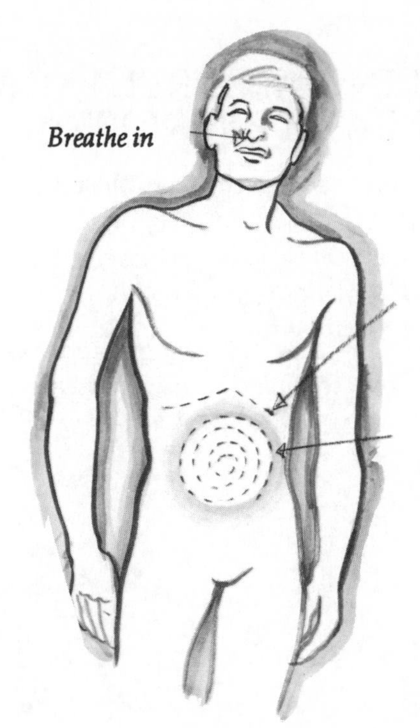

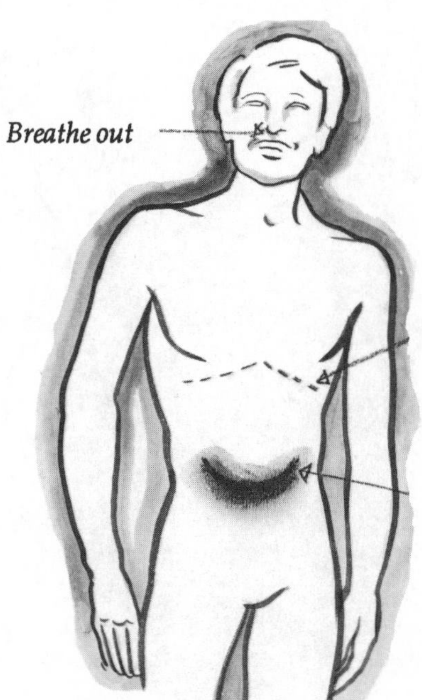

The abdominal breath

CENTRING AND RELAXING BREATH EXERCISES

All these exercises are best done with the eyes closed to aid concentration, and to cut out distractions.

Reaching the sky

With legs apart, arms by your sides, breathe in deeply as you lift the arms to a stretching position above the head. The hands are touching. Breathe out and lower the arms to the original position. Repeat this several times *slowly*.

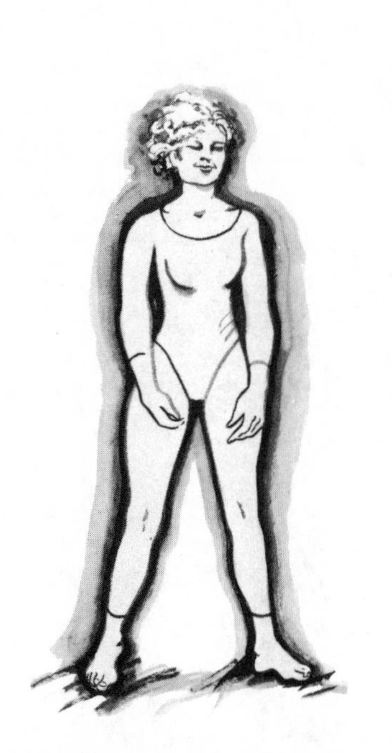

Opening and closing position

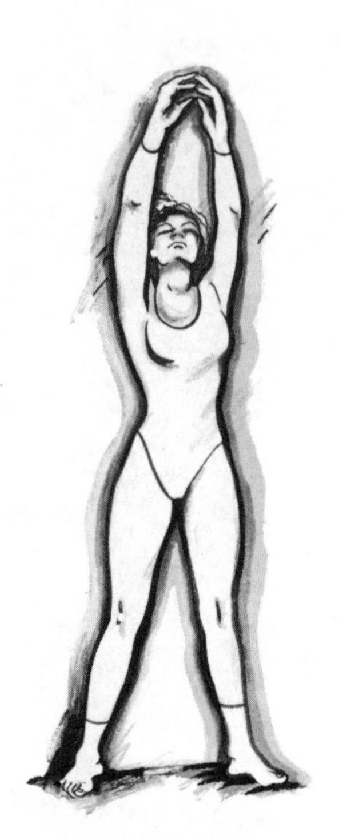

Mid position

Cross the heart

Beginning with arms stretched out in front of the chest, palms together, breathe in, opening your arms out as you do so. Bring the arms back as far as they will go, thus fully expanding the chest, and lean the head back slightly. As you breathe out, slowly bring the arms forward and cross them over the chest. When you repeat, alternately cross your arms the other way.

Starting position *Mid position* *Closing position*

Reaching sideways

Begin with legs apart, arms by your sides, looking to the front. As you breathe in, raise your right arm, reaching up and out sideways. Your left foot and hip will lift as you reach to the right. Follow the arm movement with your eyes. As you slowly lower the arm, breathe out and then repeat with the other arm. Allow the movement and the breath to flow together.

Starting position *Mid position* *Closing position*

The full yogic breath

Breathing in, bring the lower arms across each other in front of the body. As you then lift the arms and spread them out, describe a circle. When your hands reach the top of the circle above your head, begin to breathe out, spreading the arms and bending forwards, lower back first, head last.

The arms come together and cross as they sweep the floor, again with a circular motion. As you raise your body and breathe in again your hands come back to the original starting position.

1 *2* *3*

Alternate nostril breathing

This is a balancing breath used in Yoga to equalize the flow of breath into the nostrils. It has a clearing effect felt in the whole of the head and is a good exercise with which to end or begin a session.

Place the right hand over the nostrils with the last three fingers folded into the palm and the thumb and index finger extended. The index finger is in line with the nose and rests gently against the forehead. As you breathe in through the right nostril, blocking the left nostril with the folded middle finger, then close off the former with the thumb, and lifting out the middle finger, breathe out. Alternate, by then breathing in through the left nostril before blocking it off and so on.

The effect of this breath is better felt if it is done several times, say up to twenty.

THE IMPORTANCE OF STRETCHING AND YAWNING

Intersperse all the above exercises with plenty of stretching and yawning, for these are natural relaxers. Yawn and observe your body; what happened to your breath?

You will have noticed as you opened your mouth wide, what a huge gulp of air you took in and how completely you blew it out — particularly if you yawned with sound and expression! You would have felt the jaw and the cheeks stretching and then letting go; the eye muscles tightening then relaxing and the tear glands beginning to flow; the shoulders lifting and then releasing; likewise the stomach and chest. A good yawn not only releases the body from containment and inhibition, but allows it free and spontaneous expression.

Stretching is a natural way of by-passing the points of tension in the body, by fully extending the muscles past the position in which they have been frozen. As you come out of the stretch the muscles retract and loosen.

BREATHING AS A STARTING POINT FOR RELAXATION

After you have prepared yourself for relaxation and you are settled either on the floor or in a straight-backed chair, you are ready to begin to meditate. Depending upon your state of tension, it may be necessary to start at this point.

Even if you have done the previous breathing movements, you should still begin by breathing once more into the abdomen a continuous, connected, deep breath. This sort of breathing will help you to reach another level of consciousness in a very short time.

Imagine the breath as *light*, spiralling in through the crown of the head and forming a vortex as it passes down through the body. The mind should only be on the breath passing in and out of the body; don't let the mind wander to focus on your sensations or on what you think you should be feeling. You can be aware of what is happening to your body without focusing on it. If your concentration strays for a moment, gently bring it back again to your breathing, because the moment you begin to observe yourself, you create a duality. This duality separates subject from object, and thus prevents you feeling 'at one'; a peaceful unified whole.

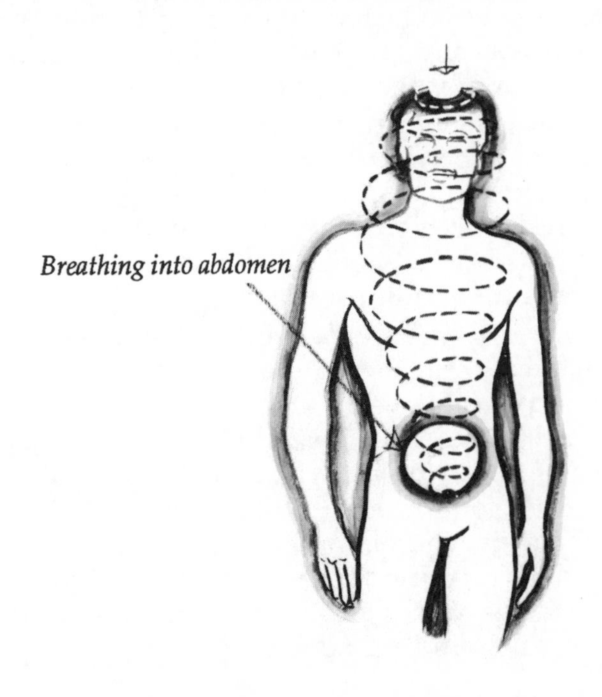

ENERGY AND THE BREATH

As you become more practised at breathing in the above ways you will realize that through the breath you can either energize or de-energize yourself, as the need arises. You will need to use your mind and your powers of visualization in combination with the breath.

To *energize* the body, imagine the light dancing, revitalizing, cleansing and renewing.

To *de-energize* the body and relax it, see the light as soothing, loosening, and use the 'out' breath (you can imagine this as a grey mist) to release and dissipate tension.

In your mind's eye, see yourself the way you wish to be — relaxed, calm and peaceful, or bubbling with energy and vitality.

Breathing to release blocked emotions

In the last chapter we discussed emotional blocks in relation to areas of specific tension in the body.

The breath too can be used most effectively to release these locked-in emotions. Lie comfortably on the floor, this time on the stomach, so that the back area (which holds most emotional tension) is free to release (use your own intuition here — you may in fact need to lie on your back if you are releasing from the stomach or arms, for example). Have your legs apart and your arms alongside your body, but not touching it; your head turned to one side. Breathe deeply and gently into the abdomen, imagining the breath as light entering through the crown of your head.

Continue to breathe like this without pausing between breaths , allowing the breath to flow easily and smoothly. After a while you might begin to notice a change in the pattern — perhaps you start to gulp or gag, or hold the breath. You may feel an uncomfortable sensation somewhere in your body. This indicates that a locked-in emotion is in the process of breaking up, and rising to the surface of the conscious mind.

It is important at this stage to *continue breathing in light*, allowing yourself to release. You may find that thoughts and images start to come into your mind. Let them come as you continue the breathing; allow whatever emotions come, to surface and be released. *Don't identify with the emotion* even though you are aware of it. Cry or laugh if you need to, but at the same time be intent on breathing out the emotion and letting it go. It is possible that you will relive a situation from the past that has caused you hurt or pain, but this time and in this state of consciousness, you have the chance to resolve the situation; the chance to look at things from a different perspective, and to come to new understandings.

As you are releasing the emotion let your body do what it needs to do — don't stop it. For example, the limbs may begin to shake, the hands open and close; you may feel an urge to arch your back and neck or shake your head; you may want to rock the whole body. If you allow this movement to happen, the body may move into alignment if it has been misaligned.

The breathing sequence for block release can thus be summarized:

1. Use the abdominal deep breathing
2. 'Breathe' in light through the crown of the head
3. 'Breathe' into the blocked area
4. Breathe out, to release
5. Breathe continuously without pause between breaths

THE MIND AND THE BREATH

You will have become aware by this time of the connection between mind and breath. In fact, this is an inverse relationship. It is not only true that the breath feeds the brain (and thus the mind) by oxygenating the blood cells but also that the mind gives greater impact to the breath.

Whenever the mind and breath coordinate, there is greater energy and power. You have only to think of a simple example to realize the truth of this statement: think how much easier it is to lift a heavy weight if your deep breathing is accompanied by a belief that you have the strength to do it.

The way we breathe is affected by our thoughts, and our feelings. If we are happy we breathe more freely and easily; if we are frightened, breathing can be interrupted, shallow and uneven.

Visualizing the breath going to a certain area of the body, seeing that area healthy and alive, is more than just imagination. As we breathe, every cell in the body is being affected and changed; as we think and feel, the body is also reacting and altering its chemical makeup. For as with life, everything connected with the body is interrelated; nothing exists in isolation.

Self Space

'I now give myself permission to create space in my day for me'

'As I breathe, so I live'

'I breathe my aliveness into my body and my life'

'My breath, my mind, my feelings, flow together in perfect harmony'

Sun circling

Sit on a straight-backed chair in the sun, with your legs apart and feet flat on the ground, palms upward on the knees, and the eyes closed. Using your inner vision, trace around the outer edge of the sun and then, as you continue with your mind to spiral into the centre of the sun, breathe it into your body through a spot between the eyebrows.

Feel, as the spiral descends to its centre, that you are pulling it into yourself, where it continues its circular movement. Feel too the health and life-giving qualities of the sun as you breathe it in deeply.

Do this for five minutes each day and accompany it with a life-giving affirmation — perhaps one of the above, or any positive statement you might choose. Notice what a difference this five minutes makes to your day, and to the quality of your living!

Colour calm

Sit outside, as for the sun circling exercise, for colour that is observed and remembered is better imagined.

Observe the colours in the landscape, with your eyes open and then close your eyes. Select a calming, restful colour: *physical* restful — green; *mental* restful — indigo, or green; *spiritual restful* — blue. Now breathe in the colour, imagining that it is seeping in through all the pores of the skin. Hold the breath for a time, to really absorb the essence of the colour, and then breathe out the breath.

Tibetan breathing

This is a centring breath practised by Tibetan monks, and sometimes also referred to as a 'Zen breath'.

The idea is to focus completely on the breath entering and leaving the nostrils, getting in touch with the rhythm of the breath, rather than visualizing its path through the body. To feel this rhythm and flow, imagine the breath as a silken thread. Notice how the breath is cooler as you breathe in and warmer as you breathe out.

After continuing this breathing for some time you will feel the mind becoming quieter, the breath becoming smoother, more automatic. Don't let the mind wander; if it does, bring it gently back to the area of the nostrils once again.

Chakra breathing

The chakras are the spiritual energy centres of the body. They originate in the etheric (spiritual) body and connect by a cord to the physical body, at various points along the spine, correlating with the nerve plexuses.

These centres rotate with energy and, depending on their state of balance or imbalance, have an effect on the health of the surrounding organs.

One of the advantages of breathing into and out from each chakra is that by doing so you become aware of the relationship between the breath and energy, as you receive feedback. You will find, as you place your hands over each chakra area, directing the breath there with the mind, that you begin to feel a response. There will be a tingling or warmth under your hands. Some of the areas will respond almost immediately; others not so readily. The response pattern reflects the state of balance in your body and as you become more sensitive you will be able to intuitively feel this.

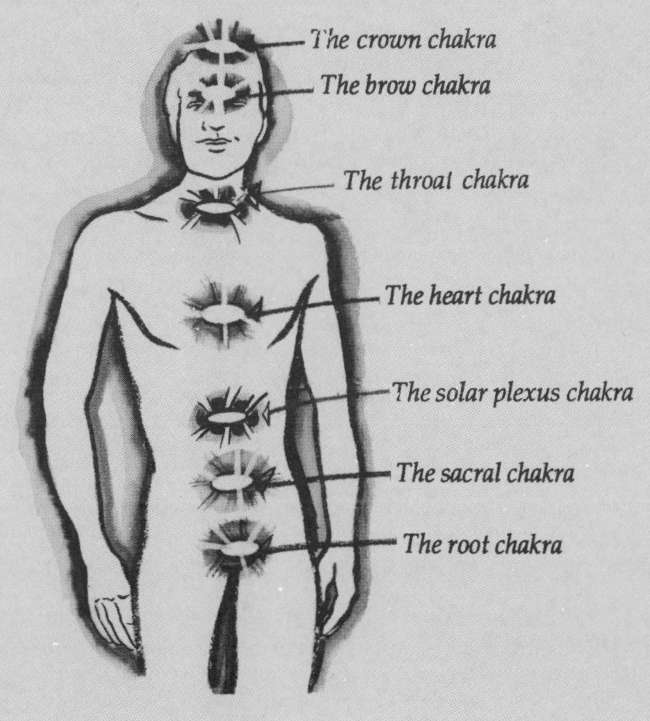

The Chakras

Right/left brain balancing

The right side of your brain governs the left (or feminine) side of your body, and the left side of your brain governs the right (or masculine) side of your body. Most people's bodies are unbalanced, one side developing at the expense of the other, and thus one side of the brain is developed at the expense of the other. Since each side of the brain is responsible for different functions, different qualities, it is important that both sides be developed. Each side can then work more effectively.

Breathing for balance

Breathe through the crown chakra and into the body, imaging the breath as light. This exercise is better done in the relaxation pose with the back on the floor, legs apart and arms not touching the torso.

Continue this deep breathing for some time till you begin to feel your body's density. Feel the balance, the relative lightness or heaviness of each side.

Now breathe into the side that feels heavier, denser, blacker, and as you continue feel it realign with the other side of your body. Begin to visualize each side now as a 'whole', seeing the harmony and uninterrupted flow of balanced energy.

See the rational, logical, specific and masculine left brain complementing the emotional, intuitive, synthesizing and feminine right brain. See integration, rather than opposition.

FOUR

Training the mind

'All of the body is in the mind. But not all of the mind is in the body.'

Swami Rama

The body and the mind are interdependent, but the mind has the ability to be in charge and to bring about changes in the body. This has been shown in numerous experiments, where people have demonstrated no ill-effects after walking on burning coals; have been able to control heart and blood vessels and produce brain wave patterns in the body at will.

One such experiment, with Swami Rama, was carried out in 1974, by Elmer E. and Alyce Green, two American scientists, who subsequently concluded:

> 'The body is only the densest section of a 'field of energy' that includes both body and mind. It is interesting to remember that our bodies, like everything else in the universe, are electromagnetic fields with swarms of particles as dense portions. We are almost entirely empty space, although we see ourselves and all nature as solid matter because this is the way we were constructed by evolution to see.
> '... For the mind is an energy structure, and *all matter, whether physiological or nonphysiological, is a matrix of energy that is somehow related to mind.* In every thought and in every cell, we are part of the general field, but we are normally unaware of this because we are not conscious of our own unconscious.' *(Misra, p.59; my emphasis - author)*

Of course, we are not all Yogis and therefore not capable of the amazing feats described above, but if we can imagine the mind in this way, composed of particles of energy, we can then see the connection with the body and the breath more easily.

Though the physiological results will not be as spectacular as those of Swami Rama, there *are* noticeable changes in the body which are common to all meditators and which have been well documented. Some of these are: lower blood pressure, slower heart beat, decreased oxygen consumption, decreased carbon dioxide elimination, and a slowing of brain wave patterns to a predominantly alpha wave.

BRAIN WAVES

It is impossible to measure degrees of calmness of mind, other than through the mind's connection with brain wave patterns. Although these patterns vary enormously with each individual, generalizations have been made about the levels of consciousness usually associated with a brain wave frequency.

Alpha is one of the four isolated patterns that has attracted much attention, as this seems to be the predominant meditative state. In the Alpha level the brain wave frequency has been measured at between 7-14 cycles per second; this is the daydreaming, reflective and tranquil state resulting from a mind that is detached, non-judgemental.

By training the mind in techniques of concentration, and letting go, the Alpha state can be reached at will.

Our normal waking state is characterized by a Beta brain rhythm, one that is above 14 cycles per second and ranges to 30 cycles per second. This is the alert, rational, analytical level; while any range of emotions can be registered at this level, it is interesting that negative emotions are not found at lower brain wave frequencies.

Theta waves, 4-7 cycles per second, while normally found in sleep, are also found in the meditative state, and in moments of ecstasy and inspiration.

Delta, 0-4 cycles per second, the slowest brain wave pattern, is associated with the deepest levels of sleep or coma.

The implications of Alpha

Our normal waking state includes millions of inputs or stimuli which we unconsciously absorb and which finally detract from our ability to see things clearly. There are just *too* many inputs, most of them not even relevant or helpful to our personal integration.

Of course it is the mind that helps us to assimilate all these numerous inputs, but why not, conversely, use it to eliminate them? If we can somehow see the mind as a director, an initiator, as being in charge, then we need no longer let things happen to us. We can use the mind to release and let go all that is unnecessary or detrimental to our well-being.

Since the Alpha state is the one in which we can see more calmly and clearly from every angle, without judgement and opinion clouding the issues, then the mind in this state has unlimited possibilities for growth and change.

Making the transition

How do we travel from a scattered, over-stimulated mind state, to one of serenity and calm? It is not easy just to empty the mind and make an instant transition! In fact, to most people emptying the mind is a frightening, impossible thought which turns them away from even attempting meditation.

In training the mind, as you did your senses, in chapter one, you can make a *bridge* from the known to the unknown. The mind bridge is **concentration**. Rather than resisting the mind, and thus creating an unnecessary barrier, make use of it to focus on an object or topic.

As the mind learns to focus it becomes calmer, increasingly more still, and thoughts no longer impinge. A state of *un*thinking is automatically reached.

CONCENTRATION

Concentration is the general state of bringing together your power and attention to focus on one point or one area. In meditation this act of concentration is sometimes given the name 'onepointedness' or 'onepointing'.

In learning to concentrate you must first improve both your powers of observation, and your memory. Some ways to do this are outlined below.

Observation

Some general steps to follow in developing the powers of observation:

1. Have an attitude of interest.

2. Make a mental connection with the object — imagine that you are flicking a switch that instantaneously connects you and the object of your attention.

3. Use your eyes.

4. Trace the shape with your eyes to imprint it on your memory.

5. Note the colour.

6. Use all five senses - hearing, seeing, smell, taste, touch - in relation to the object of observation.

7. Combine all six steps for an overview of the object.

The mental approach here is that rather than engaging your mind with the object, you become more detached, take one step back, to allow the object to 'present' itself.

Using the above steps, begin your observation with objects that are inanimate, such as a rock, a piece of driftwood, a building, a book, a statue, a machine such as a tractor or typewriter. Try to choose a variety of objects; natural and human-made, small and big, so that you really test your powers of observation. You will be surprised by what such exercises reveal about yourself as you find some aspects easier, some more difficult.

Continue with living objects such as a tree, plants, the sun, people, animals, then watch both inanimate and animate in movement, switching directly from non-moving to moving. For example: observe a yacht when still, and then when moving through water; a stone on the ground, and then in action; a tree in stillness, and then being buffeted by wind.

MEMORY

It is in remembering that the mind registers a perception and can then reflect, analyse, associate and connect.

As we observe an object and then retain it as an image in our mind, the concreteness of the image is strengthened; we make a conscious attempt to memorize, placing all our concentration on the object of attention.

In training our minds to remember, we are able to improve our powers of observation, our ability to maintain an image, our concentration.

Early writers on mind dynamics, like Jose Silva, used a system of association as a trigger for remembering events, names and numbers, learned on an 'alpha' level. The associations, called 'Memory Pegs', were visualized images that connected in some way to the object of memorization. For example if you want to remember the number TWO you might associate it with twins.

It is important that the images be as vivid and eyecatching as possible, because this is what makes them personal and unique. At the same time, the recall is more effective if the associated image is clearly expressed and not too complex; neither should it communicate contrary messages. Thus if you are to remember the number TWO, it doesn't help to visualize three two-headed monsters standing under a single tree! Your mind instantly wonders: 'Is it one, two or three, that I want to remember?'

Concentration exercise

Once you have worked on your powers of observation and on improving your memory you will be ready to try some concentration exercises. For all such exercises it is important that you first prepare yourself by assuming a comfortable position, either in a straight-backed chair (back straight, shoulders relaxed, hands turned with the palm upwards and resting on knees, legs apart with the soles of the feet flat on the floor), or cross-legged on the floor. Placing the tips of the thumb and index finger together is also a meditative practice; the upturned palms indicate a state of receptiveness, and the thumb and forefinger held together are symbolic of a turning within, and turning off to all outside stimuli.

The typical meditative pose

The cross-legged, typical meditative pose, described in Yoga as a 'half-lotus', is a common position for meditation. It can be difficult for many people, so if you prefer you can sit in a simple cross-legged position without placing the foot on the thigh.

If you decide to attempt the half lotus, first cross the legs, then place your fists on the floor behind you and lean forward, shifting the buttocks about so as to make good contact with the floor. Then lift one foot up to place on the opposite thigh (or lower onto the calf if that is more comfortable).

Your back will be gently curved rather than stiffly upright, the shoulders dropped, the head bent slightly forwards so that no strain is placed on the neck.

Breathe *in* to this position: in other words, as you breathe into the abdomen and then out, feel the body settle and relax in the position as all tensions are released.

The Candle

This concentration exercise involves a steady gazing at an object with the eyes open. When the object has been observed for some length of time and remembered, shut your eyes and internalize the image, holding it in your mind for as long as possible. As the mind image fades, open your eyes once again and recommence gazing. This exercise and others like it are sometimes referred to as *'tratak'* ('steady gazing') and always involves the same process, whatever the object. Some of these objects of concentration or meditation are discussed more fully in chapter seven.

Sit on the floor in the meditative pose (or another comfortable position) about a metre away from a lighted candle. Gaze at it steadily with the eyes open, not staring or blinking but having an attitude of relaxed receptiveness. No strain or effort need be involved.

When you feel that your eyes and your mind have absorbed the image, close the eyes and continue to see inwardly the image of the candle. Remember again not to force the image on your mind, and to continue with your slow, steady breathing. You will find that if you put too much effort into holding the image that you will tend to hold your breath as well.

If thoughts begin to distract you, bring your mind gently back to the steady gazing. You will probably notice changes in colour, as you transfer the candle image inward. The flame may darken and become more of a silhouette, as may the candle. You may see colours. Notice these things, but don't let the focus shift.

The worst trap of all is to think that you are doing well — and as you become absorbed in self-congratulation, the image disappears!

As the inner picture begins to fade, open your eyes once more and look again at the candle. Continue in this way, alternately opening and shutting the eyes for a few minutes, or at least long enough to experience some benefit. You will be able to lengthen the time for this exercise as you become more accustomed to it. Initially you may find that your eyes feel tired. If this happens, rub the palms of the hands together vigorously for a few minutes, until they feel hot, then place them over the closed eyes. You will find immediate relief, from this practice of 'palming'.

Once you have practised the Candle exercise a few times you can choose any small object, natural or otherwise, to improve your powers of concentration.

POSITIVE AND NEGATIVE THOUGHTS

Now that you have worked through many awareness exercises you will have become more sensitive to the sometimes conflicting thoughts and self-talk in which the mind engages.

The mind, being a finer part of the 'field of energy' that is the body, can vary in its level of energy depending on the nature of the thoughts held there. To divide thoughts into categories like positive or negative is of course, simplistic, since positive and negative exist more as a continuum than as isolated and separate opposites; so to banish or repress the negative is neither healthy, nor constructive.

Nevertheless, it is also true that some people seem to have a remarkably positive and balanced approach to life, while others appear to be their own worst enemies because of their negative way of interpreting their own experiences.

It *is* a matter of interpretation, and choice. While we can recognize and accept the negative within ourselves, we can at the same time choose to reflect the positive. To do this, we must be able to distinguish the difference between owning a 'positive mask' and wearing it like a street face (so that it becomes our own protection from experiencing life) and being really positive, through and through, so that it projects from the very depths of our being.

One of the sad things about negative thinking is that it becomes part of a vicious cycle, perpetuating more negativity as we constantly set out to prove our beliefs about ourselves and others. While this cycle is not a conscious process, it can be helpful to make it so and to find just how much you *reinforce* your own beliefs so that events normally turn out the way that, deep down inside, you expect them to. As Richard Bach says in his book, *Illusions*, 'Argue for your limitations, and, sure enough, they're yours! . . . The mark of your ignorance is the depth of your belief in injustice and tragedy. What the caterpillar calls the end of the world, the master calls a butterfly.'

Listen

'I can't do it.'

'I'm not clever enough.'

'I never have been a sporty person - I'm just uncoordinated.'

'I always miss out; things never go my way.'

'Other people always seem to get what they want in life.'
'I always have been shy.'
'I'm useless when it comes to fixing things - I just haven't got that sort of brain.'
'I'm always a mass of nerves when I have to get up and speak in front of others.'
'Why am I so stupid?'
'I'm such a fat slob - I hate myself!'
'I'm terrified of heights - I fell out of my cot when I was two.'
'I always make a mess of things.'

Therefore
'I'm . . .

stupid

silly

hopeless

no good

dumb

a loner

not attractive enough

not interesting enough

not intelligent enough

not exciting enough . . . '

This is a random list of judgements made about ourselves in relation to others or to our environment. The list is endless.

All the statements reflect a perception we hold of ourselves which has been internalized and generalized. It may be true that when you were two you fell out of your cot, and *were* terrified but to conclude from this, 'I am afraid of heights' both reinforces your fear in future situations and places a limitation on the development of personality.

As we continue to pass judgement on ourselves, either through self-criticism, or through imposing limitations, we are constructing a self-image that we don't really like; one that is negative. Indeed, it amounts to an overwhelming feeling, present in almost everyone to some degree, which continues to motivate our actions:

'I'm not loveable enough'

Breaking the pattern

How can you drop the destructive habits which your mind creates through its beliefs?

It's simple, but it takes persistence:

1. Recognize and examine the beliefs you have about yourself. Become more conscious of your own self-talk.

2. Reduce every generalization to a *particular* statement; e.g. 'I was terrified when I fell out of my cot when I was two.'

'I felt useless when I tried to fix . . . '

3. Add to the particular statement a 'let-out clause' that releases you from generalizing further; e.g., 'I was terrified when I fell out of my cot when I was two, *but that is in the past, and I can feel differently about heights now*'

4. Make a positive affirmation about the matter, once you have got in touch with your own fear (see 1). Repeat the affirmation often; aloud, silently, and by writing it down; e.g., 'I feel comfortable and at ease with heights — I am on top of the world.'

AFFIRMATIONS

An affirmation is a confident, positive, open-ended statement made to yourself to strengthen and reinforce your beliefs. The statement can refer to yourself or to others and it can relate to any issue that causes you concern.

Affirmations can become powerful tools for change when they are used thoughtfully, and in combination with other methods like deep meditation, in which a situation or person can be visualized. This may involve such things as regression (back to past events or to people who are now dead); or conversations with yourself or others; releasing and forgiving.

The strength of an affirmation is thus dependent on your ability to integrate it within your personality and your life. For example, it is useless constantly to repeat positive statements about being able to handle heights with confidence, if you haven't acknowledged and worked with your fear at the same time, in order to understand and then release it.

Eventually the positive statement will begin to feel a part of you and not simply be a superimposed attitude.

Using the breath in affirmation

The words we use have an energy output, as do the thoughts which we put in our heads; so that if you are seeking to replace a negative belief system with a positive one, you are also bringing about a change in energy levels. This is the energy you feel within you, and which you project to others.

You have already learned that as you feel different emotions, your breathing pattern correspondingly alters; since feelings are connected to thoughts, it follows that the way you breathe plays a necessary part in the process of affirmation.

Breath is energy; mind is energy. To take a deep breath in as you repeat an affirmation, and to hold that breath as you hold the statement sharply focused in your mind, imparts power to the affirmation.

The 'out' breath can be used to breathe out any negativity, any negative emotions.

Focusing on areas of the body

As you repeat your affirmation, breathing it into the body, you can add greater depth and power by being more specific. Breathe into the part of the body that relates to your statement; the part associated with a particular emotional or psychological quality.

In metaphysical philosophy, the chakras (see page 35), being associated with different organs of the body, are also connected with mental qualities; a balanced chakra reflects a mental balance of these qualities.

The positive qualities associated with each chakra are:

1st Chakra (root)	security, stability, strength, spontaneity, practicality, energy.
2nd Chakra (sacral)	creativity, self-confidence and optimism, patience, warmth, endurance, health, vitality.
3rd Chakra (solar plexus)	willpower, concentration, flexibility, emotional balance and expressiveness, decisiveness, self-motivation, personal power, efficiency, orderliness.
4th Chakra (heart)	joy, compassion, love acceptance, fulfilment, expansiveness, generosity, secure, nurturing.
5th Chakra (throat)	expressiveness, energy, idealism, devotion, creativity, inspiration, communication, peacefulness, loyalty, commitment, patience.
6th Chakra (brow)	imagination, wisdom, intuition, trusting, telepathy, perception, understanding.

7th Chakra (crown)	enlightenment, pure and unselfish love, creativity and manifestation, spiritual transcendence and transformation, unlimited energy, ability to synthesize, purification.

You can create an affirmation to express any of the above qualities. Breathe into the appropriate part of the body as you take your mind there, silently repeating the affirmation.

SELF-SPACE

'I am in charge of my mind, in charge of my life'

'My mind is focused and clear; my attention is total.
Nothing else matters.'

'I have within me an infinite potential.'

'I allow myself to change; I am open to the
unlimited possibilities of life.'

'I love and accept the way I am.'

'I can remember anything I choose to remember.'

Take the time to explore some of the areas mentioned in this chapter - the alpha level, concentration, memory, belief systems which affect your self-concept.
The exercises below provide a starting point.

The seven levels
Sit in your meditative pose or lie comfortably on the floor. Using abdominal breathing, progress through seven levels, beginning with the physical and ending in the alpha level of consciousness, where you feel totally at one, clear-headed and detached. Each level is associated with a colour of the rainbow and works like a trigger mechanism to bring about an instant transformation in your state of mind. The trigger mechanism effect of course, comes with continued use of the method.

The seven levels meditation

Red	**Physical** 'I am in control of my body. My body doesn't control me.'
Orange	**Emotional** 'I am in control of my emotions. My emotions don't control me.'
Yellow	**Mental** 'I am in control of my mind. My mind doesn't control me.'
Green	**Peace of mind** 'I am at peace - nothing else matters.'
Blue	**Love** 'Love surrounds me - universal, unconditional.'
Purple	**Aspiration** 'I aspire to reach my full potential.'
Violet	**'I am** in my levels.'

Focus on each colour by seeing or feeling it, breathing it into the body as you internalize and silently repeat the affirmations associated with each level.

Once you have reached the 'I am' level you can remain there as long as you like, but remember to descend back through the levels from violet to red when you decide to return to the normal waking state.

Grounding

The preparations you take to come *out* of a meditative state are just as important as those with which you begin. This final unwinding is often referred to as 'grounding'. It is essential to come back down from the Alpha level. In this case go through the colours, returning to the physical (red), when you will once more be aware of your body. In all other instances allow your breath to become more shallow as your focus returns to your physical setting. Never jump up immediately, but give yourself time. If the process of grounding is not used you could end up feeling dizzy, headachy or disoriented, quite the opposite from meditation's desired state of harmony and oneness.

Concentration and memory

Sheep in a paddock

In your mind's eye, vizualize a paddock full of sheep. Count the sheep. If you wish, this can also be a memory training exercise in which, as well as counting, you give each sheep a distinguishing characteristic and associate this with its number. For instance, number one sheep may have a long tail; number two, a collar round its neck; number three might be a black sheep, and so on.

Picket fence
Shut your eyes and imagine a blank screen on which is painted a picket fence, stretching from one side to the other. To maintain your attention, vary the width and height of the pickets as your eyes move along; count each picket.

Abdominal breath
Using the abdominal breath (see page 24) breathe in to the count of four, and out to the count of four.

Positive and Negative

The sun-moon sweep
This is a mind-breath exercise that revitalizes and energizes by instilling the positive and releasing the negative. The sun symbolizes the positive; the moon, the negative.

Lie on the floor with the legs apart; arms by the side but not touching the body, and palms turned upwards. Breathe in through the crown of the head, visualizing the breath as light, sweeping right through the body, down to the toes, bringing in a positive vibrant energy.

As you breathe out, visualize the breath as a grey colour, sweeping from the toes, right through the body, and out through the crown of the head. Imagine that you are releasing all negative energy from the body.

Affirmation mandala
A mandala is a circle with a meditative focus (see page 83).

Make your own mandala on a big piece of cardboard, filling it with a simple written affirmation and any drawings or pictures that support and reinforce the affirmation. Use colour to make it eye-catching and memorable. Meditate on it often in a similar way to the candle meditation (page 42) by alternately gazing with open eyes, then closing your eyes and holding the mental picture. Memorize the elements of the mandala, and at the same time attempt to 'feel' the words that you see in front of you: e.g. 'I love myself'.

An alternative way to meditate on the mandala, is to gaze at it constantly with open eyes and repeatedly chant the words as a 'mantra' for about twenty minutes. You will find that if you allow yourself this much time, once or twice a day, for at least a month, the words will take on a meaning and beauty of their own, as they begin to manifest their own power.

FIVE

The power of visualization

You have already encountered the word 'visualization', in reference to specific exercises in this book. We will now look more closely at visualization. What is it, and how does it connect to meditation; how do we do it, and what are its best applications?

VISUALIZATION

We can *all* visualize; we do it every day, because none of us lives entirely in the present. We therefore spend a lot of time imagining ourselves, or others, in future or past situations.

Visualization involves a seeing in our mind, as if it were real; being able to create images that are three-dimensional and alive, by using the memory (to *re-create* from the real world); the senses (to feel, see, hear, taste and smell, and thus make the inner world come alive); the mind (to connect and associate, organize, dissect, synthesize, initiate and conclude); and the emotions (to add dimension and involve our whole being in visualization).

VISUALIZATION AND MEDITATION

The eastern meditative tradition has arisen from a different culture and philosophy and therefore has different assumptions.

In the western world we also have religious traditions of meditation but these have resulted in a more rational and outer-directed approach. Because of this, most westerners find it difficult to suspend the mind and launch directly into the nothingness and stillness of the meditative state.

Visualization has thus become a popular way of occupying and focusing the mind. It can be used as a pathway to reach that inner stillness, or, alternatively, as the operative technique in a different type of meditation, called 'dynamic' or 'creative' meditation.

In 'dynamic meditation', visualization is used as a vehicle for finding out more about ourselves and others; for healing; for solving problems; for projecting ourselves into future situations, or for regressing to the past; for changing our attitudes and belief systems. Common to all these situations is the intention that *we make something happen* in the meditation, by investing an energy which creates its own momentum. The result is creative change and personal growth.

When we visualize, we use the symbolism of the mind to integrate the conscious and the sub-conscious with our higher consciousness. The process can be linked to the dream world, and to dream images, in that much of what is visualized in dynamic meditation is unconscious: it is neither planned nor intentional. And as with dreams, the images that present themselves can be interpreted.

For example, say that the regular meditation you use is a beach scene. You sketch in the familiar details — the sand, the rolling waves, the rocks and trees — and then one time you notice that an unfamiliar object has appeared in the picture. Perhaps a lookout tower has sprung up at the end of the beach, or a person walks into the scene. These extra elements seem to appear without conscious effort, and this is what makes dynamic meditation so interesting and exciting. Each new element becomes a symbol, with its own personal meaning. You interpret this by asking yourself: 'What do I associate with a lookout tower, or with the particular person on the beach?' It is useless to consult books or ask others for interpretations because the symbology relates only to your own psyche. It is formed from your experiences, associations and belief systems, and is therefore totally individual.

Initially, when you are composing a meditation scene, there will be many changes before the picture assumes some stability. This may take several weeks. It is only after your usual scene is complete, that any alterations or additions to the picture become symbols for interpretation.

How to do it

Some people find that creating a mental picture is a difficult task. The only advice I can offer is: *persist, and it will become easier*. Allow the images to flow into your mind naturally, without trying to force them in. No two people visualize in exactly the same manner, and if you *feel* a scene, rather than see it in actual colours and shapes, then that is all right too.

Free yourself from expectations and limitations. Breathe them out as you begin, by relaxing the body. As you breathe in, feel the body loosen; feel the mind becoming more open, more receptive.

Incorporate into your visualization memories of pleasant, comfortable places, and half the work is done. If you find it difficult to remember such places, establish a memory-bank by deliberately detailing a scene with your eyes open, then shutting them and re-creating the same picture in your mind. Don't turn it into a test — if you have trouble remembering open your eyes once more. After doing this a number of times you will soon find that you are more aware of what you see.

Don't get side-tracked by the details of your picture; confine yourself only to the present experience, not past memories or associations. Notice the details in your scene only to the extent that they allow you to get in touch with each of your inner senses. For example, if you are walking beside a stream, reach down and scoop up the water in your hands. Recapture in your mind the taste and texture of cool mountain water. See the sun sparkling on it; listen to its sound as it ripples over boulders and stones. Fill in your scene as completely as you can, as far as the eye can see. You may have trouble filling in the whole picture to your left or your right. This is because one side of the brain is more dominant that the other. Persist in trying to explore the empty side and you will be balancing your brain, exercising the part of it that has been under utilized.

Because of the right/left brain imbalance, you may also find that you continually 'arrive' in your scene from the one side. Don't let this bother you; as you continue with regular meditation on the same scene, you will find that this situation slowly changes. It might take weeks, months or, as in my own case, even years!

Applications of visualization

Dynamic meditation is only one type of visualization. We can also use visualization simply to reach a state of complete calm; to enable us, in combination with deep breathing, to reach an 'alpha' state. Visualization in this case is used as a *focus* for the mind, which can then let go of all other intruding thoughts without effort or intention. If the meditation is done regularly, it also becomes a *trigger* for relaxation and peace — as soon as we imagine our scene, the mind and body automatically follow suit.

It is not necessary to continue in a visualization mode. It can be used purely as a jumping off point for inner stillness and nothingness, and is much easier than attempting such a state at the outset.

The meadow

'The meadow' is one example of a particular scene which can be used, firstly to explore the inner senses, and then as a dynamic means of reaching the inner, or higher self.

I am indebted to Paul Solomon an American leader and lecturer on meditation and metaphysics for introducing me to this method of meditation, which is much more complex than my own adaptation.

His method involves using a meadow as a starting point to explore the inner senses and to leave the conscious world behind. From the meadow, you ascend a mountain, a symbol of going higher, getting in touch with the various emotional processes of change. At the top of the mountain is a temple in which the real work on the higher self is done.

While this meditation might be suitable for some people, for me it became too cumbersome and was too schematic. I felt that all the work that might be done in the temple could also be done in the meadow. It was simpler for me to visualize only the meadow, and just as beautiful and effective an experience.

Step 1. Begin either sitting or lying down, by breathing deeply into the abdomen. It may also be necessary to take yourself through a physical tension release routine, as previously described. End with the sensation of your body becoming lighter and lighter, and feel yourself float up and up, like a cloud. Imagine, as you drift towards the sun, that you are a bubble of light. You merge with the sun, absorbing its light, passing through it, on and on, till you see beneath you a meadow. Float down to the meadow, and land in it.

Look around you; what do you see? You feel the grass under your feet, between your toes; run through it, scrunch it up in your fingers and smell it. You notice a particularly beautiful tree in one part of the meadow. Go up to it — feel the texture of the bark; look at the leaves. Can you see the dappled light between them; are they moving or still? Are there any birds or animals in its branches?

Standing by the tree, you notice a stream winding its way through your meadow. Go to it. Stand on the banks and look into the water. Cup your hands and taste it; savour the taste. Follow the stream along, walking beside it. Notice how the stream changes in depth and breadth, clarity, colour. And what can you see along its banks? Stop and pick a flower; notice its shape, texture and colour. Is it perfumed? Listen for a moment to the sounds in the meadow — water rippling over rocks, bird calls, the whispering sound of a breeze through trees, bees buzzing amongst clover.

The aim is to explore, through nature, all the five senses — touch, taste, sight, hearing and smell — so that they become as real, or more real, in the mind.

Step 2 In your meadow, create a sacred sitting area. Make it special. Perhaps it is a big rock, under an ancient tree, or a grassy circle on the edge of the stream, or a more formal wooden or stone seat. Whatever it is, make it identifiable as an area of retreat.

This is the area where you can have conversations with others, or with yourself. You can invite anyone you choose into your meadow. There may be a path leading into and out of this area.

If you want to access the hidden part of yourself, you can visualize someone coming from far off, closer and closer towards you. As the person comes up to you, you realize that this is yourself, that part of you which you'd like to get to know better. You embrace. What do you feel as you do this? What do you notice? Imagine the two people merging into one. This can be a cathartic and deeply unifying experience. You can also 'talk' with yourself as a means to further self-understanding.

You may, alternatively, want to bring into the meadow someone with whom you have unfinished business; in other words, someone with whom you have been unable to sort out unsatisfactory aspects of a relationship. It may be your father, or mother. Talk with them, asking why they acted in the way they did, explaining how you feel. You will find that answers will come. The reason for this is that in the meditative state, you make contact with the 'whole' person; in such a state you are more able to see other perspectives, other points of view; more able to make connections.

Points to remember

The meadow is a place of reverence
It is not just any ordinary place, but a scene that you have invested with a special meaning. In this place you open yourself to the highest and the best; to your own radiant being. The meadow is therefore a place of outstanding beauty, a place of truth and inner awakening. Here you have the capacity to realize your own wholeness; so bring to the meadow your respect — give it your reverence.

The meadow is a private place
Feel confident that in the meadow you are safe and free to open yourself. This is a place that you have created for your own self-awakening and, providing that you observe what has been said above, the energies in the meadow will be good. You need not fear any external negative forces. It is true that in such a place you may be bringing to the surface parts of yourself which are not so pleasant, but this is just the place to explore

those areas. As you learn to own the negative parts of yourself, you will not be projecting (or attracting) these forces around you.

You are in charge here; you may invite into the meadow whomever you please. If someone appears in your meadow without your conscious invitation, know that you are free to tell them to go. On the other hand, they have probably appeared for a reason, and at some time you will need to deal with this. But remember, the choice of *when* is yours.

See the meadow in perspective
Initially, when you are creating the scene of your meadow you will need to draw in, and focus on, each particular aspect. As these become clear, it is important to bring everything together, to see each aspect in relation to the other. Stand at different points in the meadow, so that from every angle, the picture of your meadow is as complete as possible. Don't worry if there are still blank areas in the meadow — eventually you will fill them in.

Do the meditation regularly
To gain the full effect from the meadow meditation, it must be done regularly. Only in this way can a stable picture be formed in the mind; for the meadow is a land of symbols and any consequent changes have their own meaning.

For example, you may come into your meadow one day and find a fence around it, or a lookout tower that has suddenly appeared. These additions are different from whole areas that may emerge, either to the right or to the left of your picture, as you explore your meadow. In this case, think about what a fence or a lookout tower means to you — what are your instant associations? Don't intellectualize too much, or you will find yourself further away from the true inner meaning. Regular meadow meditation accelerates your growth.

AFFIRMATIONS

Visualization is most effective when used with affirmations. An affirmation is a firm and positive statement arising from a strongly held emotion. It is a way of bringing towards you the qualities and life situations you would most like to have, and to be in.

Affirmations work in conjunction with other methods to bring about a change in our belief systems — the thoughts we have about ourselves and others which condition our behaviour and help to form our self-image.

Often, when we strive and struggle to bring about change in our lives, we trip ourselves up on our own effort. Affirmation is a way around this — a mind trick, if you like.

When we make affirmations, we assume that we are already where we want to be. We suspend disbelief by already seeing ourselves as fully, clearly, colourfully, *in* the situation. We make the future the present. In this way, we release within ourselves the resistance to change; suddenly we are able to see new ways of looking at things; new possibilities opening up. It is the first step to attracting into our lives that which we really want. This process if called 'manifestation'. Visualization and affirmation are both ways of manifesting. Visualization creates the new picture in our minds; affirmation begins the new thought process — and helps to release the cycle of old thought patterns, in which we may have become stuck.

Make your affirmations powerful

Always decide on the wording for yourself. If you are to repeat it over and over again, the wording must ring true, be composed in words that you can accept and which have the best associations for you.

Make sure that your affirmation is in the present and doesn't contain an indirect negative. That is: don't begin your statements, 'I will . . .', but make them 'I *am* . . .'. Try not to word affirmations negatively, for example 'I don't need unkindness in my life anymore'. Rather say, 'I am treated with kindness and love'. Sometimes the strength of your feeling impels you to want to make such statements of aversion before the positive alternative can have an impact. Then it is better to repeat *both* statements.

Visualize the situation in which you want to be If you have a partner who is treating you unkindly, and you find it impossible to create a positive mental picture with him/her in it, then try to recapture the feeling of receiving, of being loved, respected, spoilt. Remember what it's like, and focus on it as you repeat your affirmation, either silently or aloud. As well as visualizing yourself in situations where others are kind to you, remember too to be kind to *yourself* in your daily life. If you are not, how can others know the way you would like to be treated? It may also be helpful to find a picture of a kind loving couple — put it somewhere where you can look at it often, until it is internalized and the mental picture is strong.

Repeat affirmations daily and in as many different ways as you can. Do this either by saying them in front of the mirror, by writing them down, by speaking aloud to yourself or to others, or by speaking them onto a cassette. In this way you have a greater chance of dislodging the thoughts that are already imprinted so strongly in your mind, and which you may have carried with you for many, many years.

Always accompany affirmations with breathing. Try to choose at least one time in the day when you can spend a little more time, putting yourself in the 'alpha' state of consciousness, using breathing and relaxation techniques. At other times, use your deep breathing — breathing into the abdomen, holding the breath momentarily, as you repeat the affirmation, and then breathing out, feeling the essence and meaning of the affirmation spread throughout the body. Continue this several times. Of course this breathing sequence is only applicable to silent affirmations. If you intend repeating it aloud, use the abdominal breath, breathing out as you speak. For written affirmations also use abdominal breathing, if you are comfortable breathing this way.

Put it all together

Place yourself in your usual meditation pose, either sitting or lying down, and have a book and pen beside you for later. Begin to breathe abdominally, breathing light in through the crown of the head, imagining that you are cleansing and clearing the whole body. Breathe out all tensions, blockages, toxins, negativity.

When you begin to feel still, calm and light, take a deep abdominal breath, hold, and silently repeat your affirmation. Breathe out, feeling the strength of the affirmation in your body, and then repeat the process, several times. (See page 45.)

Take a pause to ground yourself, then open your eyes, reach for your book and write a page or two of the affirmation, breathing deeply as you do so.

If you become bored with writing the one statement, phrase it in as many different ways as possible:

'I am treated kindly and lovingly.'

'I, (name), am treated kindly and lovingly.'

'Other people treat me kindly and lovingly.'

'Kindness and love are my birthright.'

'I attract kindness and love into my life.'

ACCOMPLISHING TASKS

Visualization is often advised as a method for achieving and succeeding at tasks that seem difficult, or that involve a degree of fear and anxiety.

It may perhaps be a job interview that has to be faced. What you can do is take yourself right through every imagined procedure — entering the building, the room, the first words spoken to the interviewer or panel; hearing the possible questions, and answering them confidently; leaving the room, knowing that the interview has been successful. You can call it 'psyching yourself up', but it is actually a mental 'trial run', and involves picturing yourself in the real situation, performing competently and well.

Another practical situation which might have to be faced is that of giving up smoking. Place yourself in situations that show your strength of will. Visualize yourself walking into a room where others are smoking. You feel comfortable and at ease; you may even feel an aversion to the smell and sight of the cigarettes.

In both situations, it is important to first face the fears and anxieties connected with the issues you are visualizing, to ask yourself what you are afraid of. In doing this, you are more able to set the appropriate scenes and, especially with affirmations, to make a suitable one.

The scenes you visualize, the words you repeat to yourself, have to be believable; your mind may thus need some preliminary clearing.

HEALING

Visualization has always been a big element of healing. The aim is not only to think yourself well, but to *see and imagine* it.

Selecting symbols

In America, Carl Simonton has been a pioneer in visualization techniques for cancer patients. He suggests finding a strong and powerful image to fight the cancer, which must also be pictured symbolically. Selecting the appropriate symbol may take some time, and must involve some accession to reality.

For instance, it is useless to find a puny and weak symbol for the cancer because cancer is a strong aggressor. It is an invader of cells so the image we select to combat the invader must be even *more* powerful. Perhaps it could be a white shark, eating a spreading and tentacled octopus. The white is symbolic of light and healing.

Using light

Visualize a sick person standing under a waterfall of light. See the person immersed in the sparkling, cleansing, rejuvenating, liquid light, as it falls over every part of the body; see the light also penetrating the body, flowing through. Visualize the person lighting up, becoming radiant and whole.

This visualization is particularly effective if you also imagine a shaft of light, emanating from your heart area, spreading out and enveloping the person under the waterfall of light.

As you project the light, feel an unconditional love for the person.

Note. Visualization, without the meditative state is not effective. It exists only on a superficial level and therefore doesn't bring about lasting change. Also remember, always begin with breathing and/or other techniques to quieten and focus the mind. You will intuitively know when you have reached that state of stillness.

SELF SPACE

'Visualization is natural and easy for me.'

'Perfect relaxation is mine.'

'I allow creative change to flow into my life.'

'I am the creator of my own happiness.'

'Peace and stillness reside within me.'

'My imagination knows no limits — I am free to fashion my own destiny.'

'I open myself to the wonder and excitement of life.'

Visualizing colour

Below is a meditation to free your emotional self, and to become aware of your own personal focus, your strengths and weaknesses.

In it you learn to visualize colour and will, in time, become sensitive to the differing energies of colour. Experiencing remembering improves the quality of colour. As you do, you will more easily be able to identify the colour most beneficial to your personal growth, for 'each of us, as a soul-entity, has a point of origin in one of the primary colour-rays, and our basic nature is reflected through the qualities of that particular ray.' (William David, *The Harmonics of Sound, Colour and Vibration*, De Vorss, California, 1981, p.81.)

The colours at the upper end of the spectrum are also those more conducive to meditation — such colours as green, blue, indigo, violet and of course white, which is the sum total of them all.

In the fantasy exercise set out below, the house which you imagine represents yourself. After you have taken yourself through the meditation, you will want to look at your experience more closely to see what it reveals of your own sub-conscious.

Perhaps one room was more fully furnished than the others or one room had a greater appeal to you. Maybe you found yourself going under the house — what does this represent to you? Examine, too, your impressions of the outside of the house — perhaps the windows were high up, out of reach. Again, what does this mean to you?

Directly after meditating, write down everything that you remember; only then do you proceed to analyse.

Rainbow House fantasy

First, prepare yourself for meditation in the ways previously described; you may find it easier to make a tape of the Rainbow House fantasy.

Imagine a house you'd like to have; a house where you feel comfortable, secure and safe. It can either be one you already know, or one you've dreamed up — or a combination of both.

Look at it from the outside . . . walk around it, note all its features. What material is it made from? Is it new or old? What colour is it? Turn your back on the house and look at the surroundings . . . there are a few prominent trees close to the house and, some distance away beyond the end of the garden, is a hill. Walk slowly towards it, noticing the colours around you. You reach the foot of the hill; now look back once more to the house, then bring your attention to the top of the hill.

You see a rainbow arching its way through the sky, from the top of the hill to your house. As you approach the top of the hill, you can see that this rainbow is three-dimensional — instead of it being made of bands of colour, each colour is a tube of solid yet pulsating light that you can walk into and through. You arrive and decide to explore each coloured tube one at a time — red, orange, yellow, green, blue, indigo, violet. Have fun, sliding, running, somersaulting, jumping, breathing in the different energies of each colour; find the tube in which you feel most comfortable, free, and responsive. As you step into this tube, the other coloured tubes slowly fade away and you find yourself totally surrounded by the colour that you have chosen. What are the qualities of this colour that have so attracted you? What do you feel?

Slide right down your coloured tube, enjoying the ride, till you reach your house. Step out in front of the house and this time walk inside. Go through each room, noticing all the details, the colours. Be aware of any thoughts or feelings that pass through you as you explore your house. Give yourself time here, and remember your impressions.

Now slowly you see the house fade away. Become aware of your body, wiggling your fingers and toes, shaking the arms and legs. Roll the head from side to side; blink your eyes a few times, and then stretch the whole body, stretching and stretching, yawning. When you are ready, open your eyes.

Note. This meditation is a good one to put on to tape since you will probably want to repeat it for continuing self-evaluation.

As the house represents yourself, the way both the inside and outside looks, the way you feel as you walk around it and pass through each room is important. Every detail is a symbol which reveals something about you — the symbols being the clues to a puzzle. As you piece them together you will gain an overall picture that will give you insights into your present psychological (and spiritual, if you wish to go to that depth) state.

Having said this, it is important not to approach the meditation self-consciously or with fixed expectations but to have an open, acquiescent attitude. Make only a mental note of your thoughts and feelings; don't analyze at this stage but flow with the meditation. You are more likely then to reach beyond the ego, beyond your conscious awareness.

When you repeat the Rainbow House fantasy in perhaps six months time you will be surprised at the changes revealed in yourself. The house and its rooms may have an altogether different appearance depending on the issues you are facing in your conscious life and their parallel inner connections.

Wholeness meditation

This is a structured meditation (one that defines the inner activity), involving counting and visualization in order to obtain a state of centredness. The body, mind and emotions are united in a common purpose.

Remember,don't be put off by ritual. If you can't recall the counting or the exact movements, invent your own. What remains important is the essence of the meditation — absorbing and feeling completeness, wholeness, and then projecting it, sending out love.

The counting and the sequence of movements are solely there to help you focus.

Sequence of movements

1. Begin by kneeling and sitting back on the soles of your feet with palms downward on lap. All movements between holding positions are to the count of seven; as you breathe in you count, and then hold the position as you breathe out.

2. With palms downward and index finger and thumb together, lift arms sideways to just below shoulder height. Hold.

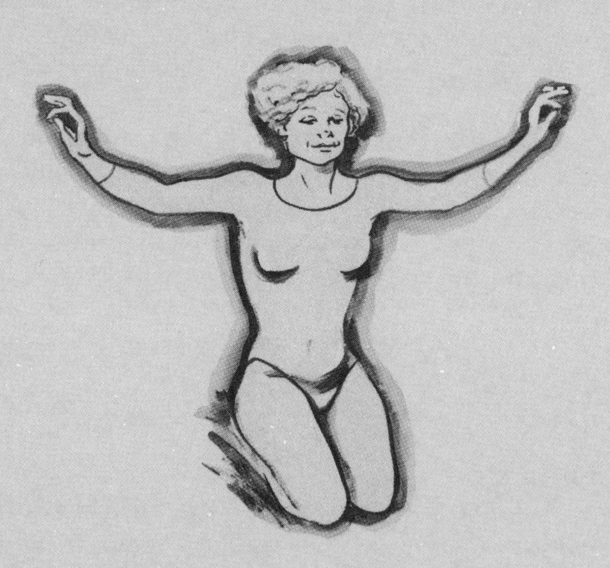

3. Move arms to just above head, with backs of hands facing. Turn hands. Hold.

4. With palms open and facing up, return arms to position two, below shoulder height. Turn hands to face downwards. Hold.

5. Move arms down so that the hands are resting at the base of the spine, one above the other. Now, for a few deep breaths, imagine vibrant, radiant light passing through the top centre of your head and down the spine to its base. On the 'out' breath, see the waste energies passing up the spine and out through the top of the head. This energy can be seen as a dirty grey colour, while the ingoing energy is white.

6. Return arms to position two. Turn palms to face upwards. Hold.

7. Move arms to position above head as in position three, with palms facing. Hold.

8. Stretch arms outwards in front to just below chest level; palms up. Turn hands down and hold.

9. Return hands to knees and hold in this position until you feel a sense of completeness and wholeness. To aid this feeling, imagine that you are a beautiful ball of light — a sun — and that light is streaming in from all directions, filling you up. Say to yourself: 'I am complete and whole.'

'I am complete and whole'

10. Turn your palms over, hands stretched open on the knees, and, both visualizing and feeling the light streaming out from your sun, say to yourself, 'In completeness I can give.'

'In completeness I can give'

SIX

Breaking down the barriers

Many books on meditation will *begin* with a chapter like this — outlining the many difficulties involved, the numerous prerequisites — and then proceed to explain the techniques.

This is offputting. Immediately, a mental barrier is created, and the reader can only see a minefield of potential dangers which contribute to the generally held perception that meditation is esoteric, removed from life.

I have already said that meditation is *easy*; that it is merely a continuation and extension of a process in which we involve ourselves every day of our lives. Within every one of us is the need for wholeness; the need to pursue it. If we approach meditation in this way, allowing our learning to flow, we will not create unnecessary resistances.

Nevertheless, now that you have had some success, now that you are familiar with ways to relax and release the body, now that you understand the dynamics of transforming and using energy, it is appropriate to address any questionings, uncertainties or recurring problems which may have arisen.

In chapter two we dealt specifically with body blocks, irritations that affect the body, and what to do about them; how to release tension and relax the body; being aware of, and able to deal with physical tensions that arise from an emotional source. This chapter elucidates some of the other related areas not previously discussed in detail.

SETTING THE SCENE

The very best way to ensure that your meditation experience is a successful one, is to begin by pre-empting the problems.

Looking forward to your quiet time, feeling *motivated* to meditate, is so important; the following are practices that will facilitate a positive experience.

Make your meditation regular. It is better to give yourself ten minutes alone each day than an hour once a week. Regularity will help to establish a routine and a mental discipline, thus making meditation an integral part of your life.

Find a quiet area in your house where you can always go to meditate. If your external environment changes too often, it provides unnecessary distraction and visual variety. Many people complain that a quiet area doesn't exist in their house. Retreating to the toilet or the bed might be your only escape — even this can work successfully if you are motivated.

More importantly, it is a case of insisting, if only for a short time, on your right to have space for yourself.

Establish a ritual. Once you have your quiet area, begin each meditation session with the same action — perhaps the lighting of a candle, or of incense; or placing before you a picture that represents peace and wholeness. You could begin with a chant of 'OM' ('O' as in home), the original mantra, meaning totality and oneness; sitting on a beautifully coloured silk scarf or piece of material; or placing in front of you an assortment of crystals. Amethyst and rose quartz (among others) when used together, help some people to achieve mental and emotional balance.

There are endless variations to the above, but the idea is to make the experience special for *you*, by investing it with your own meaning.

Meditate at the same time. As you establish a pattern of regular daily meditation, you will find that concentration comes more easily, that your willpower is strengthened, that you will better anticipate the peace and calm of the meditation experience (thus creating a trigger mechanism) if you meditate around the same time each day. Most people agree that either dawn or dusk, are good times.

Meditation at dawn. This is beneficial because you are refreshed from your night's sleep and therefore already relatively calm and relaxed. To meditate at dawn sets the tone for the day — you should feel clear headed and centred.

On the other hand, people often don't have time early in the morning because of the preparation for the day's work; others find waking early and being instantly alert, too daunting.

Meditation at dusk. The evening has the advantage of coming when the day's chores are done and mind and body can be mentally and physically released. It can be a good prelude to sleep. It can be a time to reflect on the day that has passed, and to prepare for the one to come.

Always meditate on an empty stomach. If your stomach is empty and not involved with its three hourly process of digestion, it is *quiet.* A noisy, uncomfortable, or painful stomach can be a distraction, a body attracter that hinders physical release. On the other hand the stomach must not be so empty that it rumbles as you meditate!

Don't become too comfortable. While it is not advisable for beginners to meditate on a bed of nails, neither is it helpful to be too comfortable by lying on something which is soft or moving (such as a water bed or a hammock). If you do choose to meditate on a bed, make sure that it is a hard one, and that you have enough self-discipline not to fall asleep.

Ideally, the spine should be in alignment — either sitting in a straight-backed chair, or cross-legged or lying on a carpeted floor, preferably without a pillow. If you must use a pillow, make it a small one.

MENTAL AND EMOTIONAL BARRIERS

So often, even before we begin to meditate, we set up the conditions for failure, as a result of our fears, expectations and belief systems. Reflect for a moment on your inner world, on the barriers you have created.

Below are some of the commonly voiced doubts and questions.

'What is supposed to happen?'

'How do I know that I'm doing it right?'

Be assured that there is no 'right' way, or 'one' way to meditate. What happens to you will be right for you at each particular moment in time. For example, if you fall asleep, or if your mind begins to wander off somewhere else, that is okay. There is no edict existing which says: 'The first time you meditate you should be able to . . . The second time you meditate you should be able to . . . In three months time, you should have achieved enlightenment!' If only it were so!

The only predictable thing in a successful meditation is that you will, for a fleeting moment, or for a protracted length of time, experience a feeling of supreme peace and wholeness, perhaps elation. Be your own judge. Listen to your own physical, emotional, mental indicators, and not to other people's.

The time it takes to obtain results is variable, and will depend upon your motivation and on your personal make-up. The important thing is to be constant, not to give up, and eventually, you *will* make gains — your meditation experiences will be more regularly beneficial and you will begin to notice the difference in your life.

What should I see and feel when I meditate?

Meditation, alone or in a group, is a very personal activity. We may feel the heightened energy of a group, but the way this manifests within us, what actually goes on in our minds, is related to our own personality and its associations, to our own inner symbols and the meanings which we give them.

While there *is* no universal meditative blueprint, there are some common sensations that meditators have noted, such as feelings of floating; tingling in the limbs or head; a feeling of expansion; a losing of body boundaries. If you don't have any of these sensations, it doesn't mean that you are meditating incorrectly.

What you see and feel in a meditation is also dependent on the type of meditation in which you are engaged. A dynamic meditation like the meadow, in which the aim is self-growth and understanding, will be a vastly different experience (though the end result may be similar) from a mantra-type meditation which, at its best, leads from focused concentration to a state of non-thought, non-duality and wholeness.

Meditation is something that only monks and nuns do,
in monasteries and convents.
Meditation is so esoteric — it doesn't relate to the real world.

Such statements are all too often voiced, mainly by people who are familiar with the word, but have a stereotyped idea of the activities involved.

If meditation is seen as a practice which brings about personal integration and wholeness, and adds meaning to life (as previously defined), then it automatically becomes an activity that benefits all manner of people.

Meditation is not necessarily religious; it need not have any religious content, though the continued practice of it will almost certainly lead to a greater self understanding, and to a greater understanding of the world around us.

As for its relationship to the real world — being in a calm, connected state of mind; using the whole brain; being able to concentrate and direct one's thoughts can only help, in the mundane and practical, or the more complex tasks of day-to-day life.

It is true that meditation in the past has been an esoteric practice accompanied by a certain amount of secrecy and ritual. This is no longer the case. There are many courses around, and even more books, varying from the simple and straightforward to the more complex and detailed (*see further reading*), all of which help to de-mystify meditation.

Modern -day life is too busy and fast, for people to have the time to meditate.
This is a rationalization. It is tempting to be constantly doing, constantly running, with our focus always on externals — but a balance is necessary.

Time is all about priorities — what we consider important to our lives; what matters. If something is very precious to us we don't neglect it, but rather, nurture, protect and cultivate it.

Self-respect comes in here too. Are you prepared to put other people, other jobs aside and give yourself time and space each day? Do you really need to ask others for this space? Will you *allow* if for yourself?

How do I prevent evil or negative forces taking over
when I'm in a meditative state?
The fear of being taken over is a big emotional barrier, and one that deters many people from learning about meditation.

An altered state of consciousness, such as the meditative one, makes us more sensitive, more aware, more receptive and this is where the fear arises that a stronger force will find it easy to penetrate, maybe to take possession. As has been stressed in the previous chapters, the various meditation techniques outlined also help to establish and strengthen your own control of the body, mind, and emotions. The same sensitivity referred to above acts simultaneously to protect you from negative forces since, while you meditate, you are even more acutely aware of your own identity (on a conscious, sub-conscious, super-conscious level), and cannot be so easily fooled or misled.

The attitude you bring to meditation is important. If you approach it with a sense of reverence, asking and affirming that 'good' surrounds you; visualizing and breathing in light, then you are already protected.

For an added protection, and to reduce anxiety, imagine yourself wrapped in a hooded golden cloak lined with silver. See the golden light from the cloak radiating out, and say to yourself: 'I am protected — the highest good rests within me and surrounds me'. Fear has an attracting power : over time a strong and consistently held fear creates its own thought forms that tend to highlight the objects and experiences which are feared. As you realize this is happening work on destabilizing and releasing the fears within you.

How do I free myself and at the same time maintain my identity?

If you regard the personality as an entity with certain core characteristics, and other traits that are fluid and ever-changing, then you can afford to relinquish those aspects which no longer serve you and which hold you back, while still maintaining the qualities you admire and respect.

In order to free yourself, you often have to come face to face not only with your fears, but with the unpleasant 'shadow self' (your negative part which, if unacknowledged, tends to be projected on to others). This requires an honesty, a humility, and a stilling of the ego that tends to rationalize away the truth.

If you are to come to terms with the negative aspects of yourself, you need also to suspend your self-judgement, which tends only to perpetuate the status quo: by reprimanding yourself, you may feel that you have been suitably punished and nothing more need be done. There is also the additional element of guilt, which serves only to constrain you further.

Attachments create conflict and duality

Freeing yourself is a continual process. If there are qualities within you, circumstances in your life which create conflict and strain, you cannot feel calm, peaceful and whole. The greatest causes of internal conflict are the attachments and desires which we create and hold on to.

Some of these are

- striving to make and amass *money*, for its own sake
- *gluttony*: an abnormal focus on food and eating
- an obsession with *sex* and sexual pleasure
- *possessions* and their accumulation.

Once these desires begin to own us and become the driving force of our existence we are no longer free, for we have become slaves of our own addiction. Attachments present an illusion — the illusion of happiness — but the more we chase our desires, the more true happiness eludes us. A powerful distraction is created, which prevents us from knowing our true selves.

It is through the continued practice of meditation, that we learn to discriminate between the unreal and the real, finding what matters in our lives.

When I meditate, I always seem to be looking on, observing.

This is commonly felt by beginners in meditation and relates primarily to a fear of losing control, and a fear of the unknown.

To be a little bit sceptical, a little bit cautious, does you no harm. Find out more about meditation by reading, and talking to others, and trust *will* come. Don't be pressured by others, but go at your own pace, and go only as far as you are comfortable.

Finding the balance between letting go and control is a personal thing. Your own limits must be respected but as you gather confidence in the benefits of the meditation experience, you will also come to realize that by letting go, you are not relinquishing control to some outside force, but merely freeing yourself so that a greater understanding and growth can come about. You are *always* in charge of the *rate* of that growth.

I can't seem to concentrate ... my mind keeps wandering.

A wandering mind is an undisciplined mind, and it is true that at the beginning, this is how we are. It is also true that if we *need* to concentrate, as in the case of a life or death matter, or if we *want* to concentrate, as we do when engaged in something we enjoy, then we *can* concentrate.

An undisciplined mind is a lazy mind; by doing the various concentration exercises in the book, you will find that your focus will become more one-pointed. When we are unaware, insensitive, the mind is also lazy; we haven't trained ourselves sufficiently to *notice,* and so the attention flits.

Should I 'leave my body' when I meditate?

Some people *do* leave the body behind when they meditate. This is called 'astral travelling', and should not be attempted without guidance. It is not necessary to meditation, though it can come as a result of it. Again, be warned that astral travelling can be just another distraction that takes one away from the true purpose of meditation. Examine your own motives, your own goals.

Will meditation enable me to levitate?

Of all the numerous people who meditate very few levitate — that is have the ability, while meditating, to raise their bodies to varying heights above the ground. Though I have never actually witnessed anyone levitating, accomplished meditators do claim to have done it. Levitation is a skill requiring an enormous control of bodily forces and of the surrounding energy, and is invariably accompanied by a deep personal understanding on all other levels — mental, emotional, spiritual. If you want to levitate, it will probably be a lengthy process. As mentioned in the previous question, be aware, too, of the pitfalls in making this your goal.

SELF SPACE

'My mind is perfectly concentrating.'

'I enter meditation in complete confidence - I am in charge of myself.'

'There is plenty of time to do the important things in my life - meditation is *my* choice.'

'I feel safe and protected when I meditate - I attract only the highest good.'

'I place my trust in the universe, and let go.'

'I release all attachments and desires - I am a free spirit.'

Flying balloons

To free yourself of the barriers and restrictions which you bring to meditation, try this creative visualization. See yourself in a beautiful green space, green grass as far as the eye can see. Breathe in the colour, feeling the calm and peace of greenness. You are holding a bunch of brightly coloured balloons, all with long strings. Each balloon represents a specific fear or barrier and has a keyword or words written across it. One by one, release the string of each balloon up into the air and as you see it float away repeat an appropriate affirmation to yourself, for example 'I have all the time in the world to do what I choose to do - meditation is my choice.' The keywords in this case might be 'no time'.

To make the release more effective, you might choose to see the balloons bursting and disintegrating as they drift high into the sky.

This exercise will need to be repeated several times before your particular barrier disappears.

If you find any string clinging to your hand, refusing to let go, examine the barrier you have created, getting to the root of your own fear, by asking questions as you hold the balloon. To disconnect yourself further, you may need to use a pair of scissors to cut the string.

The silver cord

If you are afraid of disconnecting from your body, or afraid of outside forces taking over, always make a visual connection, as in the case of the silver cord.

Settle yourself for meditation and begin with rhythmic, deep abdominal breaths. See the breath coming in through the crown of the head as light, and travelling through the various parts of the body, cleansing, purifying, lightening.

Go through sequentially, from the head to the toes, until the whole body is awash with light. Then feel the light gather into a beautiful big bubble, lifting from the solar plexus and attached there by a luminous silver cord.

As the bubble of light drifts higher up, the cord unravels with it. Make this your protection and feel free to float with the bubble, leaving the body behind.

SEVEN

Symbols of wholeness

As you continue to meditate, particularly if you are practising dynamic meditation, as described in chapter five, you will no doubt come across some signs and mind-pictures which continually recur. These will provide clues to the issues underlying your present life experiences. Examples of such a sign or symbol might be a tree that always appears shedding its leaves; a soaring eagle; or an eye with a missing eyeball. If you take note of these symbols and consciously use them in subsequent meditations, you will be able to work towards a greater wholeness.

For instance, take the example of the tree shedding its leaves. Perhaps you have seen it originally in your 'meadow' (chapter five). If it is still there when you return in your next meditation, you will be able to 'question' your tree. It might sound a bit ludicrous to be asking a tree questions, but keep in mind that the tree in this particular state is only a symbol which *your* mind has created. It therefore belongs not outside you, but is a part of you; a clue to the workings of your subconscious mind. You are in fact carrying on a conversation with yourself — self-questioning.

As you determine the meaning of 'the shedding tree', you may want to use it in your conscious life as a trigger for change.

SYMBOLS: TRIGGERS FOR CHANGE

When we consciously adopt a symbol, using it again and again in our daily life to reinforce a new realization, it becomes a powerful aid to achieving positive and constructive behaviour patterns. It also helps to ensure the destruction of the corresponding negative behaviour patterns.

With new realizations come new thought patterns, new emotional responses — change on every level.

In order to illustrate the value and application of symbols, let us take another example. Imagine that you are a woman who holds a memory of a childhood spent behind closed and barricaded doors, with an alcoholic father hurling abuse and hammering night after night on the other side of the door. Both the door and the room come to symbolize your protection. As you later work with this memory and its associated emotions, trying to understand your unsatisfactory relationships with men, you reach a point of no return. You feel an urgent need to release the fear that you have held of men, and to form a new relationship with them. Only in that way will you be able to attract a different kind of man into your life.

In your meditation, as you ask for release, as you ask to see things in a new way, you experience a sudden flashback. Again, you are in that childhood room, feeling the frightened emotions of the child, but this time it is different. There is another dimension. Now you have a new adult intention to face the fear and anger. While one part of you relives the frightened, angry child, the adult part detaches itself, seeking a new interpretation. Suddenly you realize what you have been doing all these years; you see that you are free to choose the qualities that you accept in a man. Just because the violence was unacceptable to you, it need not mean a total rejection of men.

Feeling empowered you unconsciously move towards the door, push aside the furniture that locked you in and, throwing the door open, embrace your father.

The opening of the door, the subsequent acceptance of the father, is a true moment of catharsis. You know that you can choose to see and respond to the good in your father and it awakens you to the possibility of a new relationship with men in general. You have a sense of freedom, a confidence in yourself — unconsciously you have liberated and come to terms with the male within.

Subsequently, this 'open door symbol' can be used on a conscious level as a reminder, every time the circumstances arise in your present life to challenge your new belief and to tempt you to act or react in the old way.

The clue to the unconscious

The above illustration shows us how symbols possess their own inner meaning, a meaning that extends far beyond a literal translation of the object, to interpretation on many levels. The symbol, then, acts as shorthand does to writing; abbreviating and condensing, providing a coded access to the inner self. It enters the conscious mind like an iceberg, with nine-tenths of its structure 'under water' or hidden. It is the vital clue to the unconscious, and helps to pinpoint our direction, to outline the journey.

ARCHETYPES, UNIVERSAL AND PERSONAL SYMBOLS

All symbols have a personal element in that they are set in the *context* of our dreams, our meditations, our lives. This context is an important factor in interpretation, no matter what kind of symbol we are dealing with.

'Archetypes' about which Carl Jung has written extensively, are unconscious symbolic representations of certain ideas (e.g. the old wise man, the great mother). These may vary in the details of their representation though they convey an essentially similar meaning or pattern. Since archetypes are not exclusive to a certain culture, time or place, they are part of a universal heritage of unknown origin, which resides in the collective unconscious of human beings.

Some archetypes representing spiritual wholeness, such as the cross and the mandala, have become 'universal conscious symbols' that are well understood. But many other archetypes that appear in dreams or meditations, may seem not to be related to the individual's life at all, and may be initially puzzling. Jung himself found surprising correlations between a patient's archetypal images and the symbols used in Greek mythology.

(See Frieda Fordham, *An Introduction to Jung's Psychology*, Pelican, 1964, p. 25.)

Unlike archetypes, 'personal symbols' are entirely individual; their meanings can only be properly interpreted by the person concerned. Their interpretation depends upon factors like our psychological make up, our life experiences and the meaning of the same symbol will therefore vary from person to person. For instance if, over time, I have had recurring unpleasant experiences associated with the sea, then any images of this represented in dreams or meditations will gain their own personal identification. The sea will be a signal for feelings of danger, pain or perhaps loss of control. To someone with a different make-up, and different experiences, the sea might be associated with excitement, challenge and adventure — self pitted against nature; or with pleasure, beauty and relaxation.

Some common symbols and their applications

The Circle

The circle is a figure of completeness, with no beginning and no end, with no sharp corners or divisions. Every outer point of the circle is equidistant from its centre.

The circle is a diagrammatic representation of the sun, worshipped by ancient people as the giver of light, life and energy. Since it has no starting or stopping point, it symbolizes the *flow* of life.

The circle represents the universe, totality, wholeness, unity; it has played an important part in both eastern and western religions, art and architecture.

The Yin/Yang circle

In this variation, Yin represents the feminine and receptive and Yang the masculine and assertive. Each contains the seed of its opposite, the seed of transformation, and together they make a whole.

The division of the circle also expresses duality, positive and negative, light and dark, good and evil and is sometimes drawn thus:

Applications

- As an exercise in concentration without staring. If the eye follows a line with no beginning and no end, first clockwise and then anticlockwise, it prevents the eyeball from staring (thus causing or aggravating tension) at a fixed space.
- Adopt the circle symbol when you are feeling scattered or divided, when you feel an imbalance between the left and right side of your body, and when you are confused by opposing thoughts or conflicting emotions.
- Visualize the circle in your waking life, using its image as a trigger for a recognition of your own wholeness. You might also repeat to yourself at times an appropriate affirmation: 'I am whole and complete'.
- Bring it into focus in your meditations, seeing yourself as the centre of a circle of light. Feel yourself radiating light like a sun, so that every shaft of light erases and eclipses all periphery visions of conflict or pain.

The mandala

The term mandala, though not exclusive to eastern cultures, is commonly associated with eastern mysticism and religion. Though the mandala is often assumed to be synonomous with the circle, it is often depicted together with a square. Within the mandala are symbolic representations of universal truths, the essence of which is the focus of the meditator. As the circle represents perfection and the divine, the square represents imperfection and the material world, the world of humanity. Drawn together they signify the union of God and human kind.

The central point of the mandala symbolically contains its realization and therefore has a special significance.

The Yantra

The Yantra is a type of mandala, usually combining geometrical symbols within a circle. Triangles, circles and squares are arranged in intricate patterns to demonstrate universal and cosmic laws.

A commonly known Yantra is that of the Tantric Buddhists, composed of nine interpenetrating triangles within a circular motif. Nine is a symbol of completion, of the end of a cycle. To the Hebrews it was a symbol of truth. The triangle with its three sides represents spiritual synthesis, the unity of body, mind and spirit; also the unity of opposites, of male and female, of the ego and the non-ego. The triangle which points upward symbolizes the reaching for the divine and the downward pointing triangle the lower nature of humans.

Applications

Along with other symbols the mandala is used as an image for contemplation. More uniquely though, it can also be used on a conscious level for self-exploration and self-expression. This use of mandalas is called 'mandala drawing', a form of diary keeping, where the information is set down not in words, but in code, in the form of symbols, shapes, and colours. As a regular method of record-keeping it can be an invaluable reference, mapping your path of self-development and growth.

It can reveal patterns of personal symbols, which by their very placement in the mandala, make connections which may not have been understood on a conscious level. The recurrence of these symbols may also provide a pointer to their importance in our lives at the time. The fact that a symbol appears again and again may also suggest, by way of urgent reminder, that we are *not* grasping a particular message.

Mandala drawing has a therapeutic effect, not only in terms of a cathartic release of emotions, but in its added capacity for bringing about new perspectives, new ways of understanding both present situations, and future directions.

As a gentle means of self-expression, it has more potential for meaning than some other forms of therapy as, for example, the release of anger into a punching bag. The fact that in mandala drawing the emotion is represented on paper (though it is spontaneous like the punching mentioned above), gives one time and distance to analyze and reflect on what is seen.

The important aspect of mandala drawing is that it must be spontaneously done, without too much thought or preparation, immediately after the body has been brought to the alpha level through meditation, and before you leave this state.

The altering of the level of consciousness, can be achieved in any preferred way:

- through music;
- through breathing;
- through mantra chanting;
- through visualization;
- through a combination of methods.

Decide on the general subject of your mandala drawing before you go into meditation. It may be

- your future direction;
- your hidden self;
- a review of your past, present, future;
- your relationship with a particular person;
- any other topic.

You may prefer to go straight into mandala drawing, knowing only your subject title, or you might choose to spend time in your meditation, on your particular subject area. The moment that you finish your meditation, open your eyes, continuing to maintain your altered state (i.e. continue your steady, deep breathing; don't allow yourself to be distracted), and *stop thinking*. Turn immediately to the paper (on which you have previously drawn a large circle), and coloured pencils, which you have placed beside you, and draw. You will have your subject in your mind, but don't reflect back to the meditation; rather, allow your expression to come from a gut, or feeling level. As you are drawing you will find that there is no 'forcing' — the images will flow almost as if you are driven by an inner voice, an inner knowing. Continue until you feel this voice 'dry up', when everything you had to say has been said.

Make sure that you then give yourself a little time to come back to the normal waking state.

To be a useful tool for self expression and self discovery the mandala drawing needs to be repeated at intervals of days, weeks or months, depending on your issue or subject.

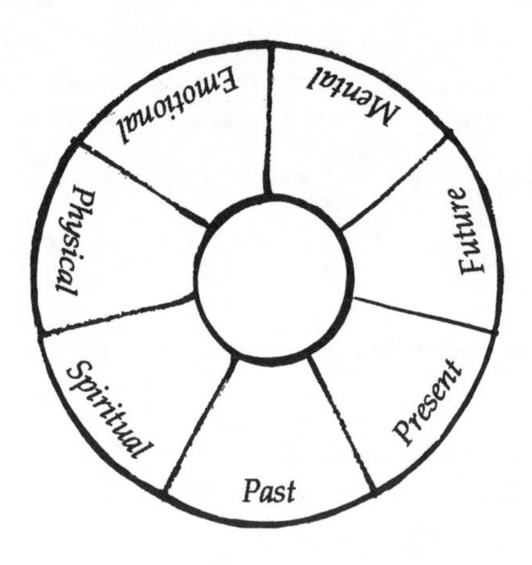

The cross

The cross has traditionally been associated with Christianity, first the equilateral or Greek cross, and secondly the elongated or Latin cross. The changing shape of the cross has parallelled the philosophical development of religion, elevating and emphasizing the spiritual ascent of humans, and de-emphasizing the material, earthly plane. Often referred to as the 'cross of light', it symbolizes the eternal link between God and humankind; spirit and matter — and therefore the 'whole'. It is a symbol of good, and has been used by man as a protection from evil; a foil for the evil forces that might be present within, or might possess from without.

Greek cross

Latin cross

The Ankh cross

This is an ancient Egyptian symbol, appearing as a 'key' and therefore signifying transformation. The key is a symbol of access to the divine, to all that is immortal, eternal. Many of the Egyptian gods and goddesses are depicted holding the ankh.

The Celtic cross

(Sometimes called the Runic cross.)
Another 'cross' variation of Viking origin, and similar to the ankh, symbolizing wholeness.

Applications
As a visual aid to crossing the boundaries between the conscious and subconscious; earthly to heavenly, or the Beta to Alpha transition.

Form the image of the cross in your mind, drawing it on your mind screen, and allowing your eye movement to finish with the vertical stroke of the cross. As your inner gaze sweeps upward, feel the corresponding spiralling energy of your breath sweeping upwards in the body, and out through the crown chakra. Repeat this sequence of breath and image till you have reached the appropriate level.

As a protective image, visualize the cross in instances where you feel vulnerable or threatened. This may apply to real life situations or in meditations when you are dealing with particular issues that you wish to resolve.

Make sure that you accompany your visualization with deep, steady breathing. Either visualize the cross before you, or incorporate your body within its image, feeling yourself a part of it. Your outstretched arms become the horizontal aspect of the cross, and the line from head to feet, the vertical aspect.

As you visualize the cross, affirm within: 'I am safe from harm. I seek only the highest good.'

Om

Om or Aum is a visual Sanskrit symbol, and also a sacred sound (ōm, as in hōme) or mantra of Hinduism. Ancient Indian texts, such as the *Mandukya Upanishad* describe the syllable 'om': 'this eternal word is all; what was, what is and what shall be.'

The long lower curve of the symbol is said to represent the dream state; the upper curve the waking state, and the curve coming in from the centre, deep dreamless sleep. The crescent signifies 'maya' or illusion and the dot above it transcendence. When you pass through the veil of illusion to the dot or circle and its associated wholeness, you are liberated from the three states and their qualities.

The mantra 'om' is also said to emanate from abstract sound and from this in turn come the seven notes of music.

Applications

Mantras must be chanted correctly as their effect lies in their vibrational quality. It is therefore important to have a teacher for this type of meditation.

The uplifting feeling that results from the chanting of 'om' is particularly felt in a group situation, but chanting the syllable alone for an extended time also brings good results. A strong resonance is felt in the body which seems to balance the energy within it, and have a calming, stilling effect on the mind.

Many people also chant with their eyes open.

The rainbow

The rainbow, made up of seven colours — red, orange, yellow, green, blue, indigo and violet — combines to form white light, representing purity or perfection. The visualization of this white light is the basis for meditation in many forms and traditions. Seven also is a mystical number, symbolic of perfect order.

RAINBOW COLOURS AND THEIR SYMBOLISM

RED	is a physical colour, a colour of excitement, of anticipation, expectation, and motivation. "I welcome change into my life and greet it fearlessly".
ORANGE	is a colour of transition, of change and release; a letting go of old patterns, habits and attitudes. An emotional colour. "I release and let go of the past; my life flows with the present."
YELLOW	is a mental colour, a colour of new life, new beginnings, of being re-born to a different reality. Entering new perspectives, new dimensions. "I allow myself to be open to whatever I might become — I am new-born."
GREEN	is a colour of peace; getting in touch with the source of life, listening to the inner voice rather than to our own egos; trusting. "Peace resides within me; I am still."
BLUE	signifies universal love; making a spiritual connection and internalizing it. Reaching beyond oneself to the universal, from the known to the unknown, and having the confidence to do it; feeling re-assured and knowing that anything is possible. "I breathe in love — unconditional, unlimited; I am confident now."
INDIGO	represents empowerment, reaching one's full potential, using the talents within. "I have the power and the ability to manifest what is unique in me."
VIOLET	'I AM'. A colour of acceptance and responsibility, accepting the consequences of one's own actions; being ready and prepared, to act with 'knowing'. "I am responsible for my own happiness — I accept my role in making it so."

WHITE	The combination of all other colours the colour of perfection, unity, oneness, purity and therefore healing.

As with sound, each colour of the rainbow represents different levels of energy, varying in wavelength and vibrational quality; these colours therefore have an effect on our own body energy and can be used in meditation for all transformational processes.

Much has been written in both popular and esoteric literature on the mental and emotional states associated with each colour; my colour assessment, (see previous page) originates from many sources, the most important of which is Paul Solomon's meditation of The Mountain (available on cassette).

Applications

Use the colours of the rainbow to bring about changes in your life. Make a 'journey' from red, through the rainbow to white, visualizing and feeling the states that each colour represents. As each colour symbolizes an aspect of the *process* of change, it is not necessary to be specific with the issue. This type of meditation, working on the general rather than the particular, sets the scene for the issue, acting as a *preparation* for real change in the individual's day to day life.

Feel the essence of the symbolism in each colour, making affirmations as you move into each new level; (e.g. violet: 'I am responsible for my own happiness. I accept the consequences of my decisions.')

It's a good idea to put on tape what each colour represents in order to help you remember the symbolism.

The six-pointed star

The six-pointed star is the union of both upward and downward pointing triangles, the union of spirit and matter. The symbol represents opposing forces, united in perfection. Also known as the Star of David and the Seal of Solomon, it is the star of universal love where the soul urge finds its place in humans. In the Hindu tradition the six-pointed star is represented by the heart chakra.

Applications

The symbol of the six-pointed star can be used in a similar way to the divided, or yin-yang circle.

As every line of the down-pointing triangle is interpenetrated and crossed by the lines of the upward-pointing triangle, this symbol more powerfully expresses the complete symmetry and interdependence of opposites in our lives. It shows the opposites not opposing, not in battle as we so often tend to see them, but in perfect balance and harmony.

Use this symbol, therefore, to give you new perspectives on your own inner and outer 'enemies'.

How to use symbols in meditation

The personal symbols that arise in meditations can be used together with the commonly known symbols mentioned above, to focus and concentrate the mind on the underlying meaning of the symbol.

Tratak

Tratak is a steady gazing. The candle exercise referred to on page XX, is an example of Tratak. Where the eyes go, the mind follows; although any of the symbols described can be entirely visualized in the mind, it is sometimes easier to have something outside the self on which to fix the attention. Look at the symbol without blinking or staring, until you can see it in your mind's eye. Then close the eyes, attempting to hold the picture as long as you can — as it fades, open the eyes again in order to re-form the mental image.

Symbols and affirmation

A symbol used in conjunction with affirmation becomes a powerful mental mantra. Here the intention is to absorb fully the inner meaning of the symbol. The constant repetition combined with complete concentration enables you to find the very seed of the thought and thus bring about transformation on many levels. For example, if you hold the 'om' image in your mind, repeating silently 'I am whole and complete' you may gain new perspectives on particular relationships, or aspects of your life which are unsatisfactory.

Tools of discovery

Personal symbols, indeed all symbols are tools of discovery. Don't be afraid to explore for yourself the symbols that emerge from meditation. In the same way that you got in touch with your senses, you can also get in touch with your personal symbols, making a bridge between the conscious and unconscious mind. Symbols are just one more pathway to the inner you. If you study them and become sensitive to their connection with your conscious waking life, you will become a more integrated person, able to anticipate the effects of your actions in the world.

As your observation sharpens, you will be able to tell when your interpretation of a specific symbol is incorrect, because it will not tally with the messages that keep returning to you as a result of your day to day interactions.

Rely on your own inituitive judgement until it disproves itself.

Symbols and the dream state

Symbols are the essence of dreams. That is why our dreams often seem nonsensical and puzzling, unconnected to real life. As we learn to interpret symbols, we also become able to interpret our dreams more readily, finding the links with our waking life.

In the state of 'lucid dreaming' these links are apparent, since the direction of dreaming can be changed, by bringing in desired courses of action or any relevant symbols.

Lucid dreaming

In lucid dreaming you are aware that you are dreaming, so it is very similar to a meditation experience.

The way to encourage this type of dreaming is to record your dreams on a regular nightly basis. Have a pad and pen by the bed, and write the dream down on the moment of waking. Don't worry about the parts that you can't remember, and don't consciously try to order your dream as you put in on paper. Write it as it comes to you.

Only when you have written it do you interpret. Give the dream a title and write down the general feeling associated with it, then look at the symbols only in the context of the dream's storyline. Their meaning is implicit there. If you try to connect to issues in your life and associations, at this stage, the meaning of the symbols will become distorted.

After you have 'listened', as it were, to the dream's message, the relevance and meaning for your own life will be more apparent. You will then be able to extract any important dream symbols for use in your subsequent meditations.

To learn more about lucid dreaming see Patricia Garfield's book, listed in *Further Reading*.

SELF SPACE

'I am one.'

'I am whole and complete.'

'I am a source for perfection — *I AM*.'

'I am a radiant whole.'

'Harmony, peace, wholeness — I am free'.

Symbols notebook

Keep a diary over a year of the various symbols which emerge from your meditations and dreams. Here is a suggested format for your notebook:

Record:

S — the symbol

D or M — dream or meditation

C — the context

I — your interpretation

O or R — occurrence or re-occurrence of symbol

T — give a title to the symbolic image

It will become abundantly clear as you continue to make these recordings, that your dreams and meditations and your daily life are inextricably linked, each one of them giving depth and meaning to the other.

Normally we see our dreams and meditations as reflections of our conscious lives, a one-way flow of communication. By keeping the symbols notebook over an extended period of time, you will begin to establish a two-way flow, where the conscious daily life in turn becomes a reflection of your dreams and meditations. The effect is to integrate and strengthen the personality, enhancing and giving direction to life.

Ordinary relationship between symbols and conscious mind

Dreams
Meditations
Reflections

Consciousness

Patchy one -way communication

Desirable relationship between symbols and conscious mind

Two-way communication
Perfect integration

Symbol pegs

Just as you established 'memory pegs' (*see* chapter four) to help you remember, so you can also use personal symbols from meditations or dreams to motivate and help you reach your goals; to affirm your values; to help you re-focus on new belief systems and thought patterns.

Every time a situation comes into your daily life that threatens to reinforce an unsatisfactory status quo, allow the symbol and its associated meaning, to flash onto your mind screen. Hold it there as long as you need, to encourage your new action, and to affirm the new direction. For example visualize a cone of light from which you can draw strength and energy whenever you feel threatened. Use it as a source of empowerment and self-assertion. Recall the symbol and its associated meaning when it is needed.

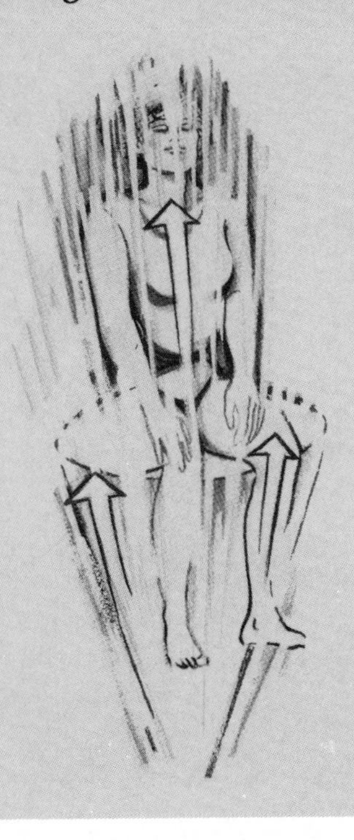

EIGHT

Synthesis
Meditation and daily life

Life is hectic for most people; time is a priority. People might not be living more difficult lives than those of a hundred years ago, but they *are* facing an accelerated pace.

There is an increased mobility available to many people in the technologically advanced countries of the world today; our expectations of what we might achieve in a day, in a lifetime, are high. The roles of men and women are also no longer easily defined, as both sexes attempt to extend and explore previously unexplored areas.

In the midst of the pace, many feel a need to find a thread to their lives that has continuity and meaning; to stop for a moment and turn from the external world of 'doing', to the inner world of simply 'being' — and then to be able to blend them together: being centred, totally present, in the midst of doing.

Achieving an inner calm and serenity in combination with a busy full, life can seem a contradiction in terms. It is a necessity to enjoying and making the most of that full life.

Reaching such a state will almost certainly involve long periods of struggle, of soul-searching, of stripping away all that is outmoded and unnecessary in one's life. It requires willpower, self-discipline and determination. Creating and exploring structures is thus often a path to a greater flexibility and freedom of expression; setting aside times in the day for meditation, practising mind and breathing exercises on a regular basis, concentrating and becoming aware of the body, can all contribute to an eventual feeling of ease; an ability to flow with life.

Bit by bit you will begin to notice that you are feeling happier and more able to cope. Your structured times for meditation are no longer so important, but your life is different.

When you wake in the morning, there are silent thoughts of appreciation for all that is good in your life. You take a few deep inhaling breaths, aware of the life force filling and rejuvenating the body.

Looking out of the window, you notice the pale hues of sunrise spreading across the sky, and the crystals of dew in the grass. You think of the things you are going to enjoy doing that day and jump out of bed with a sense of anticipation, of excitement.

While going to work, you breathe deeply, using the colours around you to energize or to centre yourself. You might also spend some of the time doing eye exercises, or repeating a silent affirmation.

You approach the car park, visualizing an empty spot just where you want it.

At work, a conflict with a colleague provides an opportunity for seeing a new perspective, or for detaching yourself from the situation so that it can be seen more clearly.

You feel a headache coming on and begin to breathe light into the head, visualizing the sharp red sensation of pain leaving the head as you breathe out.

Yes, you have come full circle. Every situation which presents itself in your life is providing an opportunity for spontaneously *living* meditation, for applying the lessons you have learnt — being aware, being sensitive to others' needs and ideas, being sensitive to your own, feeling the power of the breath, being able to visualize yourself already in the places in which you would like to be; affirming the good in your life and feeling the connection with all that is living.

This is the result of meditation; the synthesis has happened almost imperceptibly.

APPLIED MEDITATION

Once you adapt your knowledge from the structured and formal level of the trainee, and incorporate it into your daily life, you are beginning to become an 'adept' — 'a skilled alchemist' as the dictionary defines. it. Just as the alchemist transmuted base metals into gold, so you also transform the chaotic, destructive elements of your life into a meaningful whole.

Now you are practising the art of Applied Meditation! Listed below are some of the results of meditation — the spin offs.

A healthier body
A desire to nurture the physical body so that it is in balance, attuned. Since you are more aware, you don't let a state of *dis-ease* take over; you take preventative measures. As you realize your own involvement in your health, you are more prepared to assist your own preservation. You know that you are not just a physical body, that the interplay of emotional, mental and spiritual factors adds to your sense of well-being.

A growing self-respect
By listening to your emotional needs and your deepest thoughts, you learn to express your feelings, and to say what you really think. You stop judging yourself, feeling guilty, comparing yourself with others; you lose the fear of being who you are. Your greater understanding of the spiritual or higher self gives you a perspective from which to operate — loving and accepting the person you are at this point in time, and realizing your own uniqueness.

A greater regard for others
As you leave off your own self-judgement, you also judge others less; as you accept yourself, so do you correspondingly accept others.

As meditation brings a greater feeling of wholeness, you become conscious of your *links* with all other human beings. The differences and the conflict while still existing are no longer a focus — you are more prepared to resolve these so that both parties are winners, so that both retain their self-respect.

Your regard for others is an extension of your understanding and appreciation of yourself.

An awareness of the 'good' in your life
You begin to first notice, then appreciate people and things which before you ignored or took for granted.

When you no longer look back to the past or ahead to the future you are more able to focus on the good in your present life. You have an ability to leave behind regrets and not count what you don't already have. Your perspective is no longer coloured by your desires. You see things afresh, with a new joy.

An ability to live in the present
Because you are more focused, more centred, you notice more of what is happening around you. In fact, all the five senses are heightened and extended. You are more able to act, to take advantage of present opportunities, to make a better use of your own talents.

An ability to live in the 'now' imparts a wonderful vitality, a zest for life.

Being able to listen properly
Through meditation you learn to listen to others without the interference of your own ego messages.

The effect of centring enables you to focus your attention totally on the speaker, without thinking ahead to your own answers or interjections, and without straying from the subject at hand to other preoccupations of the mind.

You have also learned to accord others the respect (and therefore listening time) that you would like yourself. The ability to listen is equally applied to yourself — meditation teaches you to hear the inner voice.

Assuming self-responsibility
You come to understand the relationship between your belief systems and life experiences, and thus learn to change the self-destructive and negative patterns in your life.

You recognize that emotions are not always what you thought they were; that emotions you have felt justified in having are often a rationalization for a continued way of responding that is detrimental to relationships. The emotion becomes a screen, blocking further awareness.

By accepting responsibility for your emotions and thoughts, through meditation, you come to understand the consequences of your actions; it is only then that the outer world more closely resembles the inner world, bringing 'self' into true alignment with 'self'.

The ability to manifest
Knowing the relationship between cause and effect, taking responsibility, being able to separate ego from the true self, visualizing and affirming, being able to centre and focus are all part of the ability to *manifest* — to bring into your life that which you desire, be it specific life goals, new relationships or general approaches to living, such as the concept of 'abundance'.

The things you have always wanted in your life but couldn't reach for are now attainable.

Making decisions on life goals
Where once you were scattered, unable to follow through thoughts and actions, now you begin to join together the threads of your life into a pattern of wholeness. Your choices and decisions are thus made in terms of a personal framework; you are able to decide on the things that are important and give meaning to your existence.

As you establish priorities, you also discard all that is unnecessary and unhelpful to the attainment of your goals. Planning a strategy for achieving them is but a simple step, compared with the previous mental and emotional preparation.

A greater detachment

As you listen more often to your inner voice you are less likely to get hooked into destructive patterns of communicating with others. The greater awareness which you have developed at all levels enables you to understand the conscious and unconscious games that people play in their relationships. You are also less deceived by your own games, able to stand back from yourself and discern what is real and what is not.

Meditation teaches us to see the whole. This means that rather than interpreting the world from your own personal perspective, you are able to appreciate the total view, of which yours is only a part. Your focus shifts — once your personal reactions are not so central, you can afford to become detached. You develop a more laid back approach to situations; you are able to laugh where you formerly were unable; you can shrug off potentially hurtful or angry remarks; and you are able to feel compassion for others while not being dragged down by their plight.

Honesty

Meditation provides us with a new way of 'seeing'. As you learn to focus your attention, your sight is clearer; as you unite the conscious and unconscious parts of yourself you are more able to have an honest perception of your total self.

Self-perception increases and you *express* it by being more truthful with yourself and with the world around you. You come to realize the occasions when you have unknowingly deceived others by not being aware of how you *really* thought or felt. Your reactions have been based on your 'unknowing' and were therefore deceptive to others.

A more honest relationship with yourself brings a correspondingly more honest relationship with others.

Discrimination

Without an ability to discriminate we would not be able to make decisions about the honesty of others, about our life's goals, about what brings meaning into our lives. As we see the whole, we also see just as clearly the total contribution of its parts. We appreciate the qualities that make each part unique, yet related to the whole. Meditation teaches discernment without judgement. You can accept the differences in others, knowing at the same time what is 'right' for you. You also accept your own qualities both good and bad, and through discrimination, learn which aspects of your behaviour lead to unhappiness and which aspects create happiness.

You can release the judgement which was your former method of false discrimination, for you will see it now as both inaccurate and inappropriate.

Caring for the environment

By learning the relationship between cause and effect, which is a by-product of understanding 'wholeness', the environment assumes a greater importance in our lives. It is no longer something to be subdued or conquered; no longer something 'out there' but a part of us.

Like everything in life, there must be a natural balance where that which is taken must in some way be returned or replenished.

As meditation brings a new harmony within ourselves, we seek it too in the world around us.

Treading the path

As you continue with meditation, you will probably find many other spin-offs not mentioned in this chapter. The list is endless because your whole life will begin to change, and each change will set the ball rolling down an endless road — your path of self-discovery. With each step that you take along this road, the pathway before you will unfold and broaden.

There will almost certainly be times along the way when everything seems to close in around you, as if a fog has descended to obscure your path. When this happens, stand back, using the detachment which you have learned, and the way will open out once more for you to continue the journey.

There will be even darker times, too, when you will want to give up completely, when you will find yourself at the 'brick walls' of your life. These are the times when you are out of tune, out of balance. Force yourself then to make the mental adjustment of plugging yourself back in, connecting to a higher source so that harmony can once more flow within.

Open yourself to the unknowing so that the knowing can be found.

Don't ever give up.

SELF SPACE

'I bless every situation in my life.'

'I am willing and able to handle every situation that comes into my life.'

'I bring joy into everything I do.'

Pointers

As you incorporate each of the points below into your daily life you will find that a book like this is no longer necessary, except as an occasional reference, for you have already outgrown it!

1. Combine breathing with movement in your daily life.

2. Appreciate the people in your life both by telling them and through silent affirmation.

3. Notice and give thanks for the beauty in the world around you.

4. Make use of colour, in your surroundings and in nature, for re-establishing inner calm.

5. Listen to yourself and others, by being totally there, totally in the present.

6. Act, rather than re-act.

7. Become aware of the consequences of your own actions.

8. Learn to manifest, bringing into your life the situations and people you desire.

9. Take personal responsibility for your health and your well-being.

Some further reading

The books listed below represent a very small proportion of those which I have read. They have been valuable aids in my own self-development, and reflect the path that my interests have taken.

Meditation impinges on so many other subject areas that there is a confusing multiplicity of books on related topics: self-esteem, positive thinking, mind control, visualization, symbols, dreams. It is up to you to follow your own inclinations.

The summaries are offered as a useful starting point, since a book that is recommended is always better than one about which you know nothing.

The Art and Science of Meditation, L K Misra (Ed.), The Himalayan International Institute of Yoga Science and Philosophy of U.S.A., 1977.
A small book with chapters on meditation and the yoga tradition, obstacles in meditation, achievement in meditation; also a most interesting section on science and the super-conscious, which looks at the statements and conclusions of mystics and physicists and discusses the common ground between them.

The Art of Spiritual Healing, Keith Sherwood, Llewellyn Publications, 1985.
Discusses the relationship between disease and health; contains information on diet, nutrition and spiritual healing on the etheric level. Explains how to recognize and use the healing energy that flows through everyone, and how to remove the blockages which cause disease and imbalance.

The Calm Technique, Paul Wilson, Greenhouse Publications, 1985.
A simply written book that explains in a non-technical way the steps towards relaxation and calm. Breathing and breathing exercises form the basis for the techniques described.

The Chakras, C. W. Leadbeater, Quest, 1980.
Presents the historical and philosophical background to the chakras explaining how these spiritual centres affect both body and mind and how they can be used. Interesting photos and diagrams, and information on yantras and mandalas.

Creative Dreaming, Patricia Garfield, Ballantine Books, 1979.
Clear and simple techniques that teach you to plan dreams, control them while they occur, and integrate them into your waking life. Use of the techniques will help to improve memory, concentration and the ability to visualize. Contains fascinating information on races like the American Indian and the Senoi who have learned to control dreams and make special use of them to change their fears, and bring about emotional well-being.

Creative Visualization, Shakti Gawain, Bantam, 1982.
Describes the process of creative visualization and its many applications for dynamic meditation. Useful section on affirmation which is seen as integral to visualization. Also includes special techniques for forgiveness and release, setting goals, health and beauty, treasure maps. Full of good ideas and imaginative ways of extending the mind.

A Guide to the I Ching, Carol K Anthony, Anthony Publishing Co, 1980.
The practical companion book to *The Philosophy of the I Ching* where, by the use of 64 possible combinations, hexagrams can be created: a pattern of six broken or unbroken lines that, taken in combination, show the balance of Yin and Yang forces in any given situation. Commentaries on each hexagram provide wisdom and insight.

The Harmonics of Sound, Colour and Vibration, William David, DeVorss, 1981.
Esoteric philosophy which explores new ways of looking at sound and colour in terms of their vibrational quality. Special breathing techniques to balance the body.

Healing Music, Andrew Watson and Neville Drury, Nature and Health Books, 1987.
Explores the use of sound and visualization for health and balance. Contains creative exercises on each chakra with suggested visualizations and music. The second part of the book on new age music gives an excellent summary of albums and their particular applications.

The Healing Secret of the Ages, Catherine Ponder, Parker Publishing Co., 1981.
Catherine Ponder is an American prosperity writer and Unity church minister. She writes here of the twelve mind powers located in the nerve centres of the body. Persist through the sensationalist case histories as there is a great deal of wisdom and spiritual understanding in all her books.

The Hindu-Yogi Science of Breath, M Ramacharaka, Romford, 1960.
For anyone wanting to understand and use breathing techniques for health and meditation, this book is a classic. Philosophical as well as a practical guide.

How to Meditate, Lawrence LeShan, Bantam, 1974.
A good, basic book on meditation for the uninitiated. Doesn't go deeply into particular aspects but provides a most useful introduction. Practical and devoid of jargon.

Illusions, Richard Bach, Pan, 1978.
Another inspirational book, which in fictional form, offers insights into the ways in which we limit ourselves. The story correspondingly shows how we can free ourselves from these self-imposed limitations. Humorous but deep!

An Introduction to Jung's Psychology, Frieda Fordham, Pelican, 1964.
Distils the important theories and ideas of Carl Gustav Jung and describes the unique aspects of his psychoanalytic interpretations. For those interested in symbolism, dreams, the unconscious — a good introduction for the non-specialist reader.

Joy's Way, W Brugh Joy M.D. J.P., Tarcher Inc., 1979.
Written by a medical doctor, who after experiencing a life-threatening disease, underwent a life-changing journey of transformation. Describes his experiments with energy field-work and balancing the chakras for the alteration of disease. A subjective experience, but told with total honesty and an intellectual questioning by a professional whose conscious intention had been to remain in orthodox medicine.

Man and His Symbols, Carl Jung (Ed.), Picador, 1964.
A book aimed at non-specialists — a study of the unconscious, of symbols in terms of individualization and analysis; also explores symbolism in ancient myths and in the visual arts. Many interesting case histories on the interpretation of dream symbols.

Man's Search for Meaning, Viktor E Frankl, Pocket Books, 1963.
The personal story of an Austrian psychiatrist who, after spending three years in Nazi concentration camps, found a new approach to therapy (called Logotherapy) based on his experiences. He saw the 'will to meaning' as the primary motivational force in human beings, and the responsibility for our own happiness is connected to this. An inspirational book that represented a turning point in my own searchings.

Meditation: The Inner Way, Naomi Humphrey, The Aquarian Press, 1987.
An excellent book for those with some prior experience and knowledge of meditation. All techniques are clearly explained and placed in a historical or cultural perspective. Also includes practical exercises.

The Mystic Spiral, Jill Purce, Thames and Hudson, 1987.
Presents an understanding of the essence of meditation. The spiral, in representing a continuum, expresses the cyclic nature of time and space; it represents eternity, having neither beginning nor end. A beautifully illustrated book which shows how the symbolism of the spiral has permeated every facet of our lives. Poetry, art, architecture, philosophy, religion all provide examples of this symbol.

Natural Vision Improvement, Janet Goodrich, Greenhouse Publications, 1987.
Specifically about vision but also a holistic book with many excellent exercises and visualizations for both adults and children. Contains delightful drawings that make visualization fun. Particularly interesting right-left brain information and exercises.

The Philosophy of the I Ching, Carol K. Anthony, Anthony Publishing Co., 1980.
A wonderful book for anyone interested in exploring the nature of 'ego', of our 'superiors' and 'inferiors'. An invaluable aid to stripping ourselves of the various masks which we adopt for our own protection (and, often, delusion!).

Quiet Magic : A Fantasy. Introduction to Relaxation and Meditation for Children, Pauline McKinnon, David Lovell Publishing, 1990
An exciting and intriguing story for children. It demonstrates the value of relaxation and meditation and offers them some ways of beginning to practise these skills themselves. Useful introduction written for parents and teachers.

The Silva Mind Control Method, Jose Silva and Philip Miele, Granada, 1977.
Sets out the teachings of Jose Silva on all aspects of mind control and offers various techniques for healing, improving memory, speed learning, remembering and using dreams, self-esteem, using E.S.P.

Sources of Indian Tradition, Theodore de Bary (Ed.), Columbia University Press, 1960.
Gives an in-depth introduction to eastern religions with many translations from original source material that is unavailable in Australia. It is also a scholarly work with essays and commentaries on all aspects of both ancient and modern India.

Symbols and the Self, Violet Shelley, A.R.E. Press, 1978.
A handy little book that explains the mystical significance of symbols, and of numbers. Section on Edgar Cayce's interpretation of symbols.

Synchronicity: The Bridge Between Matter and Mind, F. David Peat, Bantam, 1987.
Explores the nature of time, chance, causality, coincidence and energy through a discussion of various scientific theories and philosophies. Also contains a fascinating section on the I Ching and how it relates to our current views of meaningful coincidence.

Theories of the Chakras: A Bridge to Higher Consciousness, Hiroshi Motoyama, Quest, 1981.
Written by the Japanese founder of the Institute for Religion and Psychology. His intensive research has attempted to use scientific parameters to document and measure the subtle energies of the chakras. Includes various exercises for increasing vitality and dissolving energy blockages.

You Can Heal Your Life, Louise L. Hay., Hay House, 1984.
An invaluable reference book which explores the correlation between disease and our mental/emotional outlook. A practical book too with many exercises on all aspects of 'change'. Based on the premise that we are 100% responsible for all of our experiences and it is we who create illness in our body, and therefore we who can heal it.

Index

HELP YOURSELF - AND YOUR CHILD - TO HAPPINESS

Pauline McKinnon

Anxiety and stress are very much part of modern living. Though stress can be a positive, creative force, it is negative stress reactions that we experience as predominant.

This book helps parents and teachers develop children's ability to manage anxiety and stress through meditative relaxation. It can be used in its own right or as a companion to *Quiet Magic* a spellbinding tale for children to read themselves. Both of these books aim to enable children to learn a way of meditating for use as a tool to make their ritual passage that bit smoother.

Pauline McKinnon has worked for the past eight years as a consultant in the Ainslie Meares form of meditation. During that time she has found that meditation has significantly reconstituted happiness for a wide range of a great many people, most of whom were formerly suffering the ill effects of stress.

215x140 mm   Paperback   128pp   ISBN 1 86355 012 7

David Lovell Publishing 308 Victoria St Brunswick 3056 Australia
Tel (03) 380 6728 Fax (03 387 1249

QUIET MAGIC: A FANTASY

Introduction to Relaxation and Meditation for Children

Pauline McKinnon

Jimmy Candlestick is a *modern* boy whose life is fast and filled with gadgets.

It is only when Jimmy falls ill and is whisked away to the country to stay with Mrs Fender that he begins to really live. When he learns to leave behind the tensions he has grown used to, adventure comes his way, along with a new sense of freedom and happiness.

Here is a story that will not only intrigue young readers but will show them the value of relaxation and meditation and offer them some ways to begin to practise these skills themselves.

> 'This book explains so much about relaxing, sitting quietly and thinking clearly.' *Elizabeth (13 years)*
> 'It steps into the world of imagination' *Paul (12 years)*

Pauline McKinnon is well-known as the author of *In Stillness Conquer Fear*. In her work as a consultant in the Meares form of meditation she has become aware of the high level of stress and anxiety in today's world. Out of her belief that prevention is better than cure, she has written this present book

215x140 mm Paperback 128pp ISBN 1 86355 004 6

David Lovell Publishing 308 Victoria St Brunswick 3056 Australia
Tel (03) 380 6728 Fax (03 387 1249

WILL YOU PLEASE LISTEN, I HAVE SOMETHING TO SAY

Jonathan Wilson-Fuller
with Sir Yehudi Menuhin

Introduction by Caroline Jones

An ABC book published by David Lovell Publishing

Jonathan Wilson-Fuller is a special person. He is someone allergic to our present-day world.

His condition restricts him to three rooms in the family home and often demands he wear a respirator. However the rooms have large windows, through which Jonathan views the world close by, and also contain books, games, materials, toys and a TV set, a window on the world at large.

Jonathan is in a unique position to show the rest of us the dangers of living on a polluted Earth. In his writing he exposes these dangers and reminds us of our responsibility to care for the world or see it perish.

'Jonathan's poems heal, teach and inspire. He sends out into a needy world this book of prophecy—the warning and the vision of a vulnerable, passionate child, who has something to say.' *Caroline Jones*

Jonathan Wilson Fuller is a gangly, freckle-faced, impish eleven-year-old. He is allergic to all food additives and to chemicals that are volatile or odorous. As a consequence he must live always indoors, breathing purified air, able to eat only a very restricted diet. For all this, he is a cheerful, lively, creative person: poet, philosopher, musician and passionate advocate of the protection of the environment.

245x175 mm Paperback 112pp ISBN 0 7333 0100 2

David Lovell Publishing 308 Victoria St Brunswick 3056 Australia
Tel (03) 380 6728 Fax (03 387 1249